A CALL TO INTERCESSION

Praying For Others: The Time is Now

ARNESTER WHITE

Contents

Acknowledgments   ix

Vision   xi

Preface   xiii

A Prayer Calling Forth Intercessors   xvii

Introduction   xix

Chapter One: An Overview of Understanding God   1

Chapter Two: Acknowledging the Holy Spirit   15

Chapter Three: The Meaning of Intercession and Intercessor   23

Chapter Four: Who Can Become an Intercessor and the Character of an Intercessor?   27

Chapter Five: The Greatest Intercessor Who Walked the Earth   35

Chapter Six: What Prayer Means in Relation to God   39

Chapter Seven: Change Your Prayer Life by Understanding the Order of Prayer   43

Chapter Eight: Reasons to Seek God's Face during Prayer   49

Chapter Nine: Preparing Our Hearts and going Before God   55

Chapter Ten: Coming Before God (Holy Hands and a Pure Heart)   63

Chapter Eleven: Praying the Solution Instead of the Problem   67

Chapter Twelve: Faith and Answers to Prayer   71

Chapter Thirteen: Some Provisions Require Fasting and Praying   73

Chapter Fourteen: Effective Divine Prayer Life (EDPL)   83

Chapter Fifteen: Examples of Effective Prayers   85

Chapter Sixteen: The Effects of Praying at an Appointed Time   91

Chapter Seventeen: Spiritual Warfare: Prayer and   93
Intercession
Chapter Eighteen: A Review of the   101
Characteristics of an Intercessor
Chapter Nineteen: Intercessor Self-Test   105

Conclusion   109
Afterword   115
Prayer For Believers   117
Prayer of Salvation   119
About the Author   121

I dedicate this book first to my Lord and Savior, Jesus Christ. He has been my intercessor, and the Holy Spirit has been my helper. They inspired me to write and publish this book. Secondly, I want to dedicate this book to my husband, Calvin, who was very inspirational and kept me focused on completing the book.

Acknowledgments

In addition to Calvin, my children, Brian and Kristen, were also instrumental in writing this book, and they often confirmed my transformation into the likeness of Jesus based on my actions. I want to thank them and let them know that they are loved. Their encouraging words and comments have helped bring me to this point in my life. I continue daily striving to be the vessel, servant, and woman of God that I have been purposed to be on this earth.

I appreciate everyone who helped and contributed to my writing this book with words of encouragement, keeping me focused and following up with me from time to time to see how I was progressing.

May God's blessings be upon each of you and may He grant you your heart's desire.

Vision

As the Holy Spirit inspired me to write this book, I could envision the opportunity to reach and teach hundreds of thousands of intercessors in the Body of Christ all over the world about the significance of prayer. Another goal I have is to reveal to each reader the importance of *effective* prayer and fasting. As righteous people, we must pray continuously to prevail and to accomplish and perfect the vision. James 5:16b says, "The effectual fervent prayer of a righteous man availeth much."

My prayer is that this book will put a hunger and thirst within each reader to go before God in prayer and to seek Him to hear His call if it is on their heart to become an intercessor or a prayer warrior. *God, may you breathe on this book, allowing it to be significant in awareness of an intimate relationship with you, calling forth intercessors and prayer warriors for the kingdom. May the Holy Spirit develop each of you to become effective in praying and warring, according to God's will, and may you also pray for others to rise up and join this ministry. In Jesus's name, Amen.*

We must always remember that "we wrestle *not against* flesh and blood, but against principalities, against powers, against the rulers of the darkness of this world, against spiritual wickedness in high places," according to Ephesians 6:12 (emphasis added). Praying is essential, enabling us to stay in God's place of rest and to be in God's peace.

I pray that this book will expose truth about prayer life, understanding of prayer, and the importance of a daily prayer life, along with reading and meditating on God's Word daily because "we are more than conquerors through Him that loved us," according to Romans 8:37.

I pray this book will unite and engage believers all over the world to effectively pray and fast for the common good with the main focus and purpose directed toward praying without ceasing always for one another (1 Thessalonians 5:17).

I pray the Holy Spirit will reveal to each reader how to pursue God's plan and save the lost.

In Jesus's name, Amen.

Let us be strong and mighty and take our position as believers and stand in the gap for one another. Be on the wall, wailing and travailing until we witness the manifestation of what God has spoken in His Word comes to pass for His people. This is needed in these times. We have an obligation to intercede and to pray for one another through the love Jesus Christ has for us as He intercedes on our behalf daily.

Preface

The book is about intercessors and intercession, but I wanted to share some things I feel are important before we begin this topic. This book is also for those who just have a heart to pray for others and to intercede on their behalf as God commands.

As you are reading, I might not seem to stay true to the title, but the book all ties together so be patient and focus on the information to get the most from the book.

I have learned that knowing who God is and knowing His character is important when praying, especially for those of us called as intercessors and prayer warriors. For example, when we need provision, we should see God as Jehovah God. When we need to feel His love as our Heavenly Daddy, we should see Him as our Abba, Father. When praying protection for others or for the nations, we should see Him as our Fortress.

The scriptures quoted throughout the book help with the understanding of prayer and provide support as written in God's Word. The Bible provides instructions about how God wants us to always be relational with Him daily, especially when praying. God has given us a handbook, the Word of truth, to tell us how to stay in our place of holiness, praying continuously. He is a God who answers prayers.

This is my first book, and it is important to me to accomplish what God has asked of me. Obedience is better than sacrifice. I have written this book in obedience, guided by the Holy Spirit, learning along the way how to please God.

We all have a divine purpose. For me, learning to seek God's face and build a genuine divine relationship with Him in my Christian walk is far more rewarding than saying "I am a Christian." Would you agree?

We were created to worship God, and a relationship with Him is the purpose of our existence. We must seek God's face and establish a relationship with Him in order to know our purpose. It is my heart's desire for each of us to be totally guided by the Holy Spirit, enabling us to walk a righteous life. We must read God's Word for our daily bread, our direction, and protection from the ways of the world. The Word is our weapon against all unrighteousness. It is "quick and powerful and sharper than any two-edged sword," according to Hebrews 4:12a. The Bible will keep us focused on kingdom living in spite of the ways and the things of the world.

We suffer from a lack of knowledge. But the Holy Spirit who reveals and brings God's Word to life releases understanding to us all through a divine, unlimited, perfect, unconfined relationship with God.

When we seek God's face to build a relationship with Him, we will discover our divine purpose for being on earth. Remember, we all have a purpose that is directed by God.

If you do not know if you are called to intercession, I recommend that you go before God and pray this prayer along with me.

Father God, who art in heaven, in the name of Jesus, I pray that the person(s) reading this book will learn to hear your voice and direction so that they can fulfill their divine purpose, especially if they are called as an intercessor, and that they will be moved by the Holy Spirit, according to your Word. I also believe that you hear our prayers when we cry out to you as David so often did.

We stand in agreement, believing you will answer us as you answered David when he prayed to you. We love You Lord, because you have heard our voice and supplications, because you inclined your ear unto us. (See Psalm 116:1–2a.)

Hallelujah! We give you praise and thanks for hearing our prayer and answering us.

In Jesus's name, Amen.

A Prayer Calling Forth Intercessors

Father God, I come before you with a heart of repentance, asking you to forgive me if I have sinned against you, knowingly or unknowingly. I forgive those who have sinned against me, and I have nothing against anyone. My heart is turned toward you, and I call upon you, my God, by faith, believing you will answer me from the heavens.

I pray that you raise up all intercessors that you have purposed for this season. I ask You to raise them up quickly and prepare their hearts so that they are focused on You as they hear Your call in this hour and obey Your command. As called, appointed, anointed, and developed intercessors, reveal to them the significance of the time and the importance of moving quickly into position of interceding for your people and the nations.

Equip and develop them, oh, God. I am trusting You. It is time for them to go forth with the power of the Holy Spirit and take their post as watchmen on the wall, intercessors, and warriors. The Holy Spirit will allow success in this calling. I ask that You pour out Your Spirit upon each person reading this book. I ask you, Father God, to convict all appointed vessels or servants who read this book so that they will take their position, trusting You and waiting for their assignment.

I give thanks unto You, Almighty God, our Heavenly Father, and by faith, I believe you have heard me and will answer. In Jesus's name, Amen.

Introduction

For whatever reason, we fail to use the Bible as we should and instead try to fix things ourselves. Most often, when we fail, we go before God. We begin to pray.

I am speaking to myself as well. I used to be like this, and I sometimes still struggle with what I consider to be unorthodox behavior. My goal is to continue daily to rid myself of acting like this and move into a place of seeking God first *always*! This means going to Him with all situations. His Word says, "Seek ye first His kingdom and His righteousness and all things shall be added unto you." (See Matthew 6:33.) This daily process must become a part of us to the point that we do it without even thinking about it.

When I pray now, I read the Bible, and I envision myself there in the moment. I actually mentally and spiritually transport to the event to get a deep understanding and experience the circumstance at that very moment. I relate the scripture with what the person I am praying about might be experiencing today. Then I pray the solution relevant to the concern found in those scriptures.

We must be honest with ourselves. Unless we can mentally and spiritually envision ourselves as a part of the scriptures and see the solution we are reading regarding the challenge or trial we are facing, we cannot understand the joy or the pain and suffering when praying. Experience by far is the best teacher. If we have not actually experienced a certain trial or circumstance, we can at least mentally picture ourselves there and depend upon the Holy Spirit to reveal truth and provide revelation. After all, He is the revelator, the one who reveals all things!

In January 2006, I was awakened in the middle of the night by the Holy Spirit, and I heard a voice tell me, "I am calling you to be an intercessor." At the time, I was not quite clear about what all of that meant to me, especially in ministry. I am still waiting on God to reveal this in its entirety, because I believe it is bigger than just praying for others.

Like most of us, I followed what I thought God was saying to me. I thought I was supposed to go to our Intercessory Ministry Team at the church I was attending at the time, my first church home. I thought I needed to be what I called the informant: someone to provide the team with prayer requests. I learned from this and want to share with you. When you hear the voice of the Lord, you should wait, be still, and ask Him questions if you are not clear on the instructions He has given you. And often we are not clear. Seek clarity on what you are hearing from God, including the what, when, and how. I know He will answer and will give you clear instructions. I am living proof of that! If He answers me, He will answer you. He is not of a respecter of persons.

Do you know we can have conversations with God? He created us for Himself. After all, we were created to be relational with God, our Heavenly Father. Genesis tells us how important we are to Him through Adam and Eve.

When I acknowledged being an intercessor, I thought my church intercessors would do the praying for me and all I had to do was provide the names of the people and their concerns. And that would be that. At the time, I did not know what intercession truly meant or what the calling of intercession was. I had failed to ask God for clarity and details and had not waited for the rest of His instructions. Instead, I jumped ahead of God and went off on what I thought it meant based on my intellect. Sound familiar?

Needless to say, working as an informant never occurred. I was so far from the truth! This is a perfect example of completely missing out on God's purpose for your life. I did not have clarity, and I put my own thoughts into what I was hearing. We must remember, "His thoughts are not our thoughts." (See Isaiah 55:8a.)

I later received a prophecy about being an intercessor, which took five years to manifest in the natural realm. It did not occur at the church I was attending at the time but was birthed and developed in me after I left. You see, I was instructed by the Holy Spirit to attend my current church, and I was also told this is where my gift(s) would be further developed. At the time, I was not even aware of the gifts, and I certainly had no idea what they entailed or what that all meant. But from past experience and spiritual growth, I knew it would be wise to wait and allow the Holy Spirit to guide me.

I discovered then that we all have a lot to learn about
God and who He is to us. I believe if we would all be honest
with ourselves, none of us are scholars with degrees in this
area. We certainly don't know all about God in His fullness.
And most of all—I am talking to myself here—we are
learning to hear and obey His voice, learning to wait for the
Lord and act upon His command by reading the Word and
hearing Him when He speaks.

The most important part of our walk with God has been
and should be building a genuine divine relationship with
the Father, Jesus, and the Holy Spirit. We learn to go before
God prayerfully to know Him as our supernatural God and
Father.

We should not just know Him for what He does for us or
go to Him for the stuff He can give us, as one of my church
members commented in class one day. God is available to be
intimate with us. He is not just a God who gives and gives
and gives. Even so, His Word says, "If ye shall ask anything
in My name, I will do it" (John 14:14).

We all have a purpose on earth. You need to ask yourself
if you are willing to let go of your will and pursue God's will
for your life on this earth. This will be reckoned when you
decide to commit and not compromise yourself by going
against His will for your life. Giving up our will takes time
and will not happen overnight. We must gain patience and
endure unto the expected end. Your destiny, calling, divine
purpose, and very life depend upon it. I want what God
wants for you.

As an intercessor, my heart's desire is that all God's children be blessed and fulfilled in their destiny; and above all,
that they love one another. Love is one of God's greatest
commands. Love will cause us to stand in the gap for one

another. Love will cause us to sacrifice ourselves and go up and war in prayer for our family—neighbor, church member, the lost, or complete strangers—no matter what they have done. This demonstrates a true example of the genuine love of Christ within us.

Do you think we can get to a point where we will pursue such a strong walk with God that we always pray (communicate and connect with God) for those we barely know or for those who have wronged us? I believe in my heart that as called intercessors, we must do that if we want to please God and be in His perfect will.

In God's presence, we find time to pray, war, praise, and worship, which depends on how the Holy Spirit guides us.

Chapter One: An Overview of Understanding God

If we are to grasp the importance of effective praying, strategic interceding, and warring for one another, we must realize the importance of establishing a genuine, divine relationship with God. I say this because many of us say that we have a relationship with God, but as time progresses and as our lives become busy, we start questioning our walk with God and start searching our hearts. But I believe that when we read God's Word, we discover that we really do not have the relationship with God we think we had or would like to have with Him.

A revelation of our Heavenly Father is very important in discovering who God is to us and understanding His character and personality. We must understand that a genuine, divine relationship with God is a deep relationship that cannot be touched or tampered with by anyone or anything. It is the anchor that secures us and keeps us on solid ground. It cannot be shaken or disrupted, and our relationship is solid as a rock. This divine relationship with God allows our prayer life to elevate and intimately experience God. John 14 expresses the intimacy God requires of us as His creation. "And I will pray to the Father, and he shall give you another Comforter (the Holy Ghost), that *He may abide with you* forever. Even the Spirit of truth, whom the world cannot receive, because it seeth Him not, neither knoweth Him not; but ye know Him, for *He dwelleth with you and shall be in you*" (John 14:16–17, emphasis added).

First and foremost, a relationship with God can only be built and based on *faith*. "Now faith is substance of things hoped for, the evidence of things not seen" (Hebrews 11:1). God is *not* seen.

"The just shall live by *faith*" (Romans 1:17b)

Let me use an analogy that we all can relate to because we are visual. If we want to establish a closer relationship with someone: family, coworker, business partner, associate, friend, or others—we must learn the intimate things about that person. How can we do this with God? Read His Word and pray for revelation and understanding, asking God to reveal Himself to us.

Exodus 33:13a says, "Now, therefore I *pray* thee, if I have found grace in thy sight, shew me now thy way, that I may *know* thee, that I may find grace in thy sight" (emphasis added). This scripture tells us that we can ask to know His ways.

This was my first step. I desired and wanted to know God and His ways so that I could truly learn to love Him. I wanted to obey God and be favored by Him. I wanted to know Him as God and all His characteristics. I believed He would answer my prayers.

I decided to search the scriptures and meditate on His Word. As I did this, I realized the Holy Spirit started guiding and exposing the true living God to me, a God of *impossibilities* and *possibilities* at the same time. This was quite an amazing revelation for me! "For with God nothing shall be impossible" (Luke 1:37) and "with God all things are possible" (Matthew 19:26b).

God has revealed Himself to me as an omnipotent God. Omnipotent means having great or unlimited power.[1] What a great description of God's character! I asked myself, "Who is God to me?" I realized that knowing who God is has contributed to making me the person I am today.

He is Jehovah God, the provider of *all* my needs. I am not ashamed to say, "He is everything to me." As Christians, we should see God as Jehovah. Yes, this book is about prayer, but to understand prayer, as mentioned earlier, we must understand God and who He truly is to us. He is not just words written in the Bible. He is so much more.

Most people think that God is only a being who allowed His Son, Jesus, to die on the cross for us so that we could be saved. But salvation is actually the beginning of a *new life*. God, the person I have grown to know, is much more than the all-powerful being who offered me salvation through his only begotten Son.

I pray that each person who is reading grasps the revelation of God with the help of the revelator, the Holy Spirit, bringing each person to a different level that will change their lives forever.

We must understand the actual character of God as opposed to seeing God as the one who gives, and we just stop there.

Our God wants us to spend time with Him and communicate with Him intimately through worship, which includes fellowship and trusting and following Him daily! First John

1:3 says "that which we have seen and heard we declare to you, that *you also may have fellowship with us*; and truly *our fellowship is with the Father and with His Son Jesus Christ*" (emphasis added). This scripture tells us that God's desire is to fellowship with us.

Fellowship means communion or friendly relationship.[2] I prefer the definition of communion a word most Christians can relate to easily. We often have communion during church service. Communion means an act or instance of sharing intimate fellowship.[3] These definitions align with my revelation. God wants us to spend time with Him.

God is genuinely continuing to draw closer to us, to contact and stay in touch with us. We need to do the same. We need to genuinely continue to seek Him and draw close to Him. I believe it begins by *desiring* a genuine, intimate relationship with Him and being willing to consistently stay in touch and connected to Him daily. We can start by reconsidering where we stand with God regarding our relationship, especially the quality and quantity of time we spend with God during our appointed prayer time.

James 4:8a (NKJV) says, "Draw near to God and He will draw near to you." These two things: humility before our God and connection with Him will allow us to always be lifted up by Him. He will allow us to victoriously rise above our circumstances!

Do you truly see God as God? He is the "I Am" God. God said to Moses in Exodus 3:14, "I AM THAT I AM; and He said thus shalt thy say unto the children of Israel. *I AM* hath sent me." He cares for us. Do you see Him as one who cares for you? Do you see Him as Emmanuel, always with you? He takes care of you whether or not you realize it.

The Bible has many verses that remind us that God will

not forsake us. "And the Lord, He it is that doth go before thee; He will be with thee, He will not fail thee, neither forsake thee: fear not, neither be dismayed" (Deuteronomy 31:8).

Our God is always there for us. We are the ones who turn away from Him. He will not force His *will* upon us but gives us a choice to accept and love Him or deny His existence. Next, I'll talk about God, the Father, the Son, and the Holy Spirit as the Trinity.

The Trinity

We must identify with the Trinity: God, the Father; Jesus, the Son of God, and the Holy Spirit. I have learned the three have a unique purpose in our lives and should be treated and acknowledged as such. We are joint heirs with Christ.

It is easy to emphasize Jehovah, our God, and minimize Jesus, bearer of salvation, and the Holy Spirit, our teacher and guide, in our daily walk. I am consistently developing a genuine, intimate relationship with all three persons in the Trinity and coming into a deeper realization that I must learn to become intimate and cooperate with them all, learning and defining which one is communicating because the three commune with me if given the opportunity. They correspond with us at any given moment. We must train and fine tune our spiritual perception for clarity.

We must be able to recognize who is communicating and obey their instructions or commands.

Based on my experience in my early walk with the Lord, many churches did not teach about the Trinity, but this doctrinal truth is evident in the Bible. The three are one and are very real in our lives as believers. First John 5:7–8 says,

"For there are three that bear record in heaven, the Father, the Word (Jesus), and the Holy Ghost (Holy Spirit): and these three are one. And there are *three* that bear witness in earth, the Spirit, and the water, and the blood: and these three agree in one" (emphasis added).

After I read these scriptures and now that you have read them, hopefully you agree. The truth of the Trinity is evident! I am sure you noticed that the Holy Spirit is a part of the Trinity. We have the Trinity available to us every day. It is our choice whether or not we submit.

The Holy Spirit is the "Spirit of truth". He is our Comforter and our Guide, and He helps us walk out a righteous life. More importantly, the Bible tells us that the Holy Spirit is our promise from God. If God references the Holy Spirit as a gift and a promise to us, I see His Word as meaningful.

The revelation I received as time passed about the significance of the promise in my life was how essential the Holy Spirit is to me. I realized I needed to acknowledge His presence and gain understanding of how to submit to Him daily, especially when praying, because He is my helper in prayer. I will talk in depth about the Holy Spirit later, because I believe the Holy Spirit is a key in prayer and when praying.

God as Jehovah

Psalm 83:18 says, "Men may know that thou, whose name alone is Jehovah art the most high over all the earth." As Jehovah, He is with us, provides for us, protects us, helps us, and heals us. He is truly everything to us and is definitely for us. He is Jehovah-Jireh, our provider. He always provides. Genesis 22:10–14 mentions that God provided a sacrifice for Abraham to replace Isaac when Abraham offered Isaac up for a burnt offering.

Always remember, "God is our salvation." Isaiah 12:2 says, "You will trust, and not be afraid; for the Lord Jehovah is our strength and our song; He also has become our salvation."

God Is Love

We must understand God is love, and God's love is unconditional. It is called *agape* and means the love of God or Christ for humankind, brotherly love, unselfish love the highest of the four types of love in the Bible.[4] First John 4:8 says, "He that loveth not knoweth not God; for *God is love*" (emphasis added). This scripture really struck me when studying about God. He is clearly stating that if we do not love, we do not know Him! I had to really examine myself as a believer after digesting this scripture.

I spent a lot of meditation and time on this passage. If love was not evident in my life toward others, I honestly could not say "I know God" and if I do not know Him, then I do not love Him either. This was a wake-up call for me. I believe it is almost impossible to love someone unless you are consistently involved with that person on a personal level.

When we go before God in prayer, know that His agape love which is God's unconditional love covers a multitude of sins. God forgives. We must learn to forgive ourselves and others. Proverbs 10:12 says, "Hatred stirreth up strifes; but love covereth all sins."

Remember, we have God 's unconditional love so that when we lose hope and feel that there is no open door for us, a door for *prayer* is always open. We can receive power at the mercy-seat of God because of His love toward us.

God is love, and He sacrificed his Son, Jesus, so that we could live with Him forever. Ask yourself how you feel about your sisters and brothers in Christ in relation to this kind of love.

Can you put aside emotions, cares, and concerns and put others first? Do you pray for others even though you feel swayed to pray for yourself? Do you show genuine love toward others—no matter their race, creed, or color—the way God does toward us?

Son of God, Jesus, Our Savior

Jesus Christ, our Savior, is the Son of God, an example of God's love as mentioned earlier. He is the bearer and deliverer of God's love. Jesus came, lived, suffered, and died to glorify the Father so that it can be seen and known on earth how glorious our Father's love is toward us. In John 3:16, God clearly shows us that Jesus is an example of how much He loves us. In order to love someone, you must be interactive with them and give of yourself.

Romans 5:8-10 also tells us that "God commendeth His love toward us, in that, while we were yet sinners, Christ died for us. Much more then, being now justified by His blood, we shall be saved from wrath through Him. For, if when we were enemies, we were reconciled to God by the death of His Son, much more, being reconciled, we shall be saved by His life." I think you will agree with me that these scriptures are evidence of God's love and that Jesus is our Savior!

As we are convicted of our flaws in relation to our faith

in Christ, we understand that believing in Him requires yielding our whole heart, life, and will to Him. We should receive a revelation that we should strive to be humble, which is what I started working toward.

I also believe that we must receive revelation that we are to desire to become full of humility. Humility or meekness is the opposite of pride, which will lead us into *the unity of full faith in Christ* so that we individually and corporately may receive the fullness of God in our lives.

Ephesians 4:13–14 states, "Till we all come in the *unity of the faith* and of the knowledge of the Son of God, unto a perfect man, unto the measure of the stature of the *fullness of Christ* that we henceforth be no more children, tossed to and fro, and carried about with every wind of doctrine, by the sleight of men, and cunning craftiness, whereby they lie in wait to deceive." (Emphasis added).

Remember, Jesus is our pathway, and more importantly, He is essential to us developing a genuine, intimate relationship with God!

God as Our Father

God is Abba, our Father in heaven. Here are two scriptures confirming God as our Father. First Corinthians 8:6 tells us, "There is but one God, the Father, whom are all things, and we in Him; and one Lord, Jesus Christ, by whom are all things and we by Him."

Genesis 1:26 is provided for reference recognizing God as our Father when we go before Him in prayer. The word image in the world is referenced as DNA. I believe that we attained God's DNA within us when we are born again, a new creature in Christ Jesus, and we are His, and He is ours.

Here is the actual scripture: God said, let us make man in our image, after our likeness, and let them have dominion over the fish of the sea, and over the fowl of the air and over the cattle, and over all the earth, and over every creeping thing that creepeth upon the earth. Genesis 1:26

Ask yourself when you go before God during prayer if you see and know Him as your Father who hears the cry of His child. If not, you should. He is our Father just as we are His children.

When perceiving God as our Father, we can expect His help in our lives. By acknowledging we are His children, we should depend upon Him. He is our Abba Father, and He is always there for us, as it is written in John 16:23b, "Verily, verily, I say unto you, whatsoever ye shall ask the *Father* in my name, He will give it you."

Remember Romans 8:16–17 "the Spirit itself beareth witness with our spirit that we are the *children* of God. (Emphasis added). And if children, then heirs; heirs of God, and joint-heirs with Christ; if so be that we suffer with Him, that we may be also glorified together."

No matter what the concern is, knowing we are God's children, we are to go before Him with faith, believing, and pray the answer in His Word, reminding Him of His promises because He is our Father and His promises are truth.

We should not go before Him crying and whining about our problems; instead we should focus on the solution. Yes, we should acknowledge our concerns, which He already knows, or we can just start off by saying, "Our Father, who art in heaven, I know that according to your Word in

Matthew 6:7–8, you already know my needs." Then immediately pray the answer or solution to what you are going through, according to God's Word. Pray the answer in the scripture in regards to the concern, believing the solution will overcome the concern. Have faith.

An example of faith is praying to God for lack of rain and it does not rain for three years and six months. Faith is when rain is needed and you pray for rain to grow the crops and rain comes down upon the earth as mentioned in James 5:17-18. I will be discussing more about Elijah's faith later which will include the scriptures. We should not allow fear, doubt, or unbelief to sway us from our faith.

God as Our Friend

Most people I have talked to about being a friend of God really had to give this some thought. So did I. Seeing God and Jesus as my friend was a challenge. Friendship with God is a special relationship. Proverbs 22:11 says "He that loveth pureness of heart, for the grace of His lips the King shall be his friend."

God desires to be friends with us. Abraham shows us how important friendship is to God. Abraham was known as "a friend of God". God offered His friend a blessing: to be the *father of many nations*. What a wonderful friend He can be to us all!

Genesis 17:1–5 says, "When Abram was ninety years old and nine, the Lord appeared to Abram, and said unto him, I am the Almighty God; walk before me, and be thou perfect. And I will make my covenant between Me and thee, and will multiply thee exceedingly. And Abram fell on his face: and God talked with him, saying, As for Me, behold, My covenant is with thee, and *thou shalt be a father of many nations*. Neither shall thy name any more be called Abram, but thy name shall be Abraham; *for a father of many nations have I made thee*" (emphasis added).

Remember, Abraham was God's friend, and we are earthly descendants of Abraham, decreed by God as the *father of many nations*. Romans 4:16–17a mentions, "It is of faith, that it might be by grace; to the end the promise might be by grace; to the end the promise might be sure to all the seed; not to that only which is of the law, but to that also which is of the faith of Abraham; who is the *father* of us all. (As it is written, I have made thee *a father of many nations*.")

We can be relational and considered friends of God. If God was so generous with Abraham, who is known as His friend, how much more generous will He be with each of us as His heirs and joint heirs with Christ Jesus? After all, we are His sons and daughters *and* His friends. This is certainly something to think about and meditate on. It was definitely a stunning revelation for me. What an awesome God we serve! His examples of love are always amazing!

At this point in the book, we have had an opportunity to search our hearts and our minds and ask ourselves who God really is to us. This revelation and understanding will tie into my next comment. By *faith*, I believe God is Love, Jehovah, Father, and Friend. By faith, I believe He gave His only begotten Son, Jesus, and He left us the gift and promise of the Holy Spirit to help us pray and live a righteous life. We *must believe* that when we *pray,* God hears our *prayers,* and we *must have faith; believing* that God will also answer when we pray "in Jesus's name." First John 5:14–15 tells us, "This is the confidence that we have in Him, that, if we ask anything according to His *will*, He heareth us; And if we *know* that He hears us, whatsoever we ask, we *know* that we have the petitions that we desired of Him" (emphasis added). Mark 11:24 (KJV) tells us, "What things so ever ye desire, when ye pray, believe that ye receive them, and ye shall have them."

I believe that quoting these scriptures daily is a start for any believer who wants to grow on the path to maturity in faith according to God's Word. I am not an expert; I just believe.

By doing this, I have come to realize who God is to me on a much deeper level. My desire to know Him in His fullness has also intensified. Proverbs 4:7 says, "Wisdom is the principal thing; therefore get wisdom; and in all thy getting get understanding." This is such a powerful scripture!

I should *not underestimate my walk with God.* I should *not take Him for granted.* I can confidently share with you through wisdom and understanding that I truly trust God in my life more and more every day.

I hope after reading this chapter, you have received revelation and have a better understanding that God truly is our God if we will allow Him to be. This is essential to a successful prayer life. It is either His will or yours; it cannot be both! We do not want to be double-minded people. The term "double minded" comes from the Greek word *dipsuchos,* meaning a person with two minds or souls.[5] We must submit either to the mind of Christ or to the mind of the flesh. The mind of Christ always follows God's will.

---

1. "Omnipotent," dictionary.com, accessed September 7, 2018, https://www.dictionary.com/browse/omnipotent?s=t.

2. "Fellowship," dictionary.com, accessed September 7, 2018, https://www.dictionary.com/browse/fellowship?s=t.
3. "Communion," dictionary.com, accessed September 7, 2018, https://www.dictionary.com/browse/communion?s=t.
4. "Agape," dictionary.com, accessed September 7, 2018, https://www.dictionary.com/browse/agape?s=t.
5. "1374. dipsuchos," biblehub.com, accessed September 7, 2018, https://biblehub.com/greek/1374.htm.

Chapter Two: Acknowledging the Holy Spirit

"I indeed baptize you with water unto repentance; but He that cometh after me is mightier than I, whose shoes I am not worthy to bear; He shall baptize you with the *Holy Ghost (Holy Spirit)* and with *fire.*" Matthew 3:11 (emphasis added).

Receiving the Holy Spirit is essential for us all, especially for intercessors which will be explained in the next chapter. The Holy Spirit knows how to pray and what to pray, as discussed earlier. The point of this chapter is to establish that we must depend upon the Holy Spirit to help us go before God in prayer, not praying repetitious prayers as the Pharisees did, but effectively praying with purpose and strategy, expecting God to hear and answer! If you have not yet received this revelation, I recommend that you pray as I did to receive revelation of Matthew 3:11. I am sure your prayer life will definitely change. Mine did drastically.

In this chapter, we will spend more time discussing the

Holy Spirit, the third person of the Trinity. Now, let us ask "who is the Holy Spirit?"

If we are to understand how the Holy Spirit helps us, we must understand who He is. The Holy Spirit is our gift and promise. First Corinthians 6:19–20 says, "Our body is the temple of the Holy Ghost which is in us, which we have of God, and we are not our own. For we are bought with a price: therefore glorify God in our body, and in our spirit, which are God's." The Holy Spirit is significant in our prayer life.

Our Intercessor

Paul talks about the Holy Spirit as our intercessor who intercedes on our behalf during prayer. He intercedes and prays through us, which cannot be expressed in words. Romans 8:27 states, "He that searcheth the hearts knoweth what is the mind of the Spirit, because He maketh *intercession* for the saints according to the will of God" (emphasis added).

The scripture tells us we must pray in the spirit, which is orchestrated by the Holy Spirit, because the Holy Spirit knows how to pray. I do not believe we can pray unto God effectively without the help of the Holy Spirit.

Our Revelator

Let me reiterate. When we pray in the Spirit, God reveals through the Holy Spirit, our revelator, things to come and things related to the answer we are seeking in prayer.

First Corinthians 2:10 says, "God hath *revealed* them

unto us by His Spirit; for the Spirit searchest all things, yea, the deep things of God" (emphasis added).

Our Comforter

John 14:26 says, "The *Comforter*, which is the Holy Ghost (Holy Spirit), whom the Father will send in my name, He shall teach you all things, and bring all things to your remembrance, whatsoever I have said unto you" (emphasis added).

Our Guide

John 16:13 tells us, "When He, the Spirit of truth, is come, He will *guide* you into all truth: for He shall not speak of Himself; but whatsoever He shall hear, that shall He speak: and He will shew you things to come" (emphasis added).

Our Helper

Romans 8:26 says, "Likewise the Spirit also *helpeth* our infirmities: for we know not what we should pray for as we ought: but the Spirit itself maketh intercession for us with groanings which cannot be uttered" (emphasis added).

Many people believe that praying in a certain tone or with dramatic gestures contract God's attention. I used to believe that as well, but I discovered that is not true. Instead, it is all about connecting with God by abasing our flesh and going before God "spirit to spirit".

I believe we should always remember to pray in our "unknown tongue" (which is praying in the Spirit and with the Holy Spirit), which allows our spirit to connect with

God and pray to God. The Holy Spirit prays to God on our behalf. He knows exactly what to pray and how to pray for us. I believe praying in the spirit allows us to block out all human flesh, including emotions. This allows our spirit to align with God's Spirit, and we pray with the Spirit of truth.

I have witnessed many prayers being answered based on this method of praying. I am not saying all of my prayers have been answered by praying with the Holy Spirit because God answers in due season, but my results are far greater than they were in the early days of my walk with God which is also contributed to the intimate relationship I have with God now.

By faith, I do believe that the other prayers will be answered as well. I want to ensure I am clear. I am not saying that God does not answer prayers if you do not do this or if you do that. But I am saying God has order in everything, including prayer.

God has provided us with a guide to godly living, the Bible. I know that if I go outside of God's Word, doubt might creep in, which is not of God; therefore, I ensure I am aligned with the order of God when going before Him to make known my prayer or petition.

Our Indwelling Helper

I would like to recap: if we search the scriptures, we will find the Holy Spirit is significant in many ways; He is designed to benefit us in our walk with God in heavenly places. The Bible mentions the third person of the Trinity, the Holy Spirit, as our indwelling helper, who helps us pray and knows what to pray.

Being interactive with the Holy Spirit is vital when

communicating with God during our daily walk, especially when it comes to prayer. In today's climate, the Body of Christ must search for spiritual excellence to be "filled with the Spirit of God, His *indwelling* within us" (emphasis added). Ephesians 5:18 commands us, "Be not drunk with wine, wherein is excess; but be filled with the Spirit."

I believe a part of God's plan was making sure we had help in walking out a righteous life here on earth. Therefore, after Jesus ascended into heaven, He gave us another precious gift, the Holy Spirit, to reveal to us how to live a righteous life in the earth as believers. He teaches us how to go before God in prayer.

We must learn how to closely connect with the Holy Spirit and how to submit ourselves unto Him. Once we release (abase) our flesh and submit to the Holy Spirit, we can and will let Him guide, direct, inspire, and strengthen us and pray with us and through us. I believe this can be accomplished by allowing the Holy Spirit to provide us with revelation from God's Word.

Remember, the Holy Spirit is also the interpreter and revelator of God's Word, and as called and chosen intercessors by God we must learn how to pray with Him.

We must allow the Holy Spirit to enlighten our mind. Enlighten means to give intellectual or spiritual light to; instruct; impart knowledge of what we should pray.[1] In my personal experience, when I allow the Holy Spirit to enlighten me, He shows me what I need to pray and a strategy to use as well.

Renewing the mind is through the Holy Spirit at God's command. When I allow the Holy Spirit to begin to move within me and renew my mind, I begin to understand God's will and to pray according to His will.

We must allow the Holy Spirit to help by putting the right words in our mouth, which are often unexpected or unknown to us in our minds because our spirit man is connected with the Holy Spirit (abiding as one), not with our flesh. First Corinthians14:15a Paul says, "I will pray with the spirit and I will pray with the understanding also."

Praying in the spirit or in our "unknown tongue" allows our spirit to communicate only with God without involving the flesh. First Corinthians 14:2a Paul says, "He that speaketh in an unknown tongue speaketh not unto men, but unto God." We must pray to God, not man, when praying. God doesn't notice the outer man but the inner man, according to 1 Samuel 16:7b, which says, "The LORD seeth not as man seeth; for man looketh on the outward appearance, but the LORD looketh on the heart." We want to pray from our heart, not our mind.

Is it not wonderful to know that we are praying to a living God who knows our struggles? He assures us that our prayers will be answered as we walk in righteousness before Him.

We should be accountable for what God asks of us, such as keeping and obeying *all* His commandments and not indulging in sin; especially if what we are asking of Him and expecting of Him to answer our prayers.

The Holy Spirit must be present in our prayer life. Just think about this for a moment: Do you think that one reason for unanswered prayer is that you do not welcome the Holy Spirit in your life to guide you, especially in prayer? God's Word tells us that the Holy Spirit knows how to pray, but if you have not included the Holy Spirit and allowed Him to lead you in prayer, you might not have known His place in prayer. Or you might not have believed in Him. In Romans 8:26, it is expressed that the Holy Spirit is our helper "Likewise the Spirit also helpeth our infirmities: for we know not what we should pray for as we ought: but the Spirit itself maketh intercession for us with groanings which cannot be uttered." I have read this scripture for years, and it is quite evident to me that the Holy Spirit is real and important in our prayer life.

Allowing the Holy Spirit to help us pray is important in regards to making sure we address all areas of concern and every circumstance in prayer. He is our indwelling helper, and we should take heed and take advantage of His presence within us to improve and perfect our prayer life with God.

In the past, I often did not know what or how to pray regarding a particular situation. I started seeking God and expressed a yearning and desire to know my Father, Jesus, and the Holy Spirit in their fullness. I soon learned that I needed the Holy Spirit to help me pray. I had read this in God's Word, but somehow I had not received revelation of it, even though I had received the Holy Spirit. I realized I had to be wise and understand what involves the will of God when I go before Him. I knew this could only be perfected in me through the Holy Spirit.

When I allow the Holy Spirit to lead me in prayer, I hear direction from God that sometimes includes how to resolve my concern. I call this being positioned to receive your answer when requesting God's help about a certain matter or person. So far, I must say that this has worked in my prayer life far beyond what words can explain.

First Corinthians 15:31 mentions our flesh dying daily. How can this happen if we do not constantly regret our sinful behaviors when we are convicted of them? The Word of God tells us that we must ask for forgiveness when we have participated in any unrighteous actions.

We must precisely understand that we cannot do anything in our strength, no matter how much we think that we are in control. I always like to keep myself in check by saying, "Hey, if you were in control and could do whatever you wanted to do to change your life, why your life the way it is and not how you want it to be?" I then quote this cliché as well. "To thine own self be true." (This is a quote from Shakesphere in "Hamlet").

We all, at one time or another, have envisioned our lives differently than what they are. I always smile or laugh out loud when I repeat this to myself. But on a serious note, reminding myself of this quickly humbles me. No matter our beliefs, we need to receive revelation that we are *not* in control!

I want to end this chapter by saying that it is my heart's desire that "we will always pray everywhere, lifting up holy hands, without anger or doubt," according to 1 Timothy 2:8.

---

1. "Enlighten," dictionary.com, accessed September 7, 2018, https://www.dictionary.com/browse/enlighten?s=t.

Chapter Three: The Meaning of Intercession and Intercessor

P raying is the foundation of our Christian walk and a main component of being a Christian. In Matthew 6, during the Sermon on the Mount, Jesus prayed what has come to be called the *Lord's Prayer*, which I will discuss later in the book. This is considered the model prayer of the Christian faith and shows us how to pray for others.

As we discussed earlier, intercession means an act or instance of interceding.[1] Intercession is someone pleading with God on behalf of another or others who desperately need His intervention. Intervene is the root word of intervention, which means to come between.[2] Intercede is the root word for interceding, which means to act or interpose in behalf of someone in difficulty or trouble, as by pleading or petition and also means entreaty in favor of another, especially in prayer or petition to God on behalf of another.[3]

We must understand intercession and intercessory praying in their completeness. It is written in James 5:16 that we "confess our faults one to another, and pray one for another, that we may be healed. The effectual fervent prayer of a righteous man availeth much." This scripture validates our need to all pray for one another, and it provides the result and the power of praying for one another.

An intercessor is one who takes the place of another or pleads another's case through prayer. This also means a person who is praying or presenting a petition to God on behalf of the person or persons.[4] This is also referred to as standing in the gap. Intercessors are called or raised up by God but cannot succeed in this calling or ministry without the Holy Spirit. In order to understand a calling, you must understand what the calling means and entails. From first-hand experience, we need two major components to perform God's will in ministry: revelation and understanding. While there are others, I will focus on these two as they relate to intercessors.

We can acquire revelation and understanding through wisdom. We need the wisdom of God to have a successful walk with God in our lives, relationships, and ministry. We must be wise men and women of God to carry out God's blueprint in every area of our lives. Wise individuals refer to Ecclesiastes from time to time to understand the season of a situation in your life. "For God giveth to a man that is good in His sight wisdom and knowledge, and joy; but to the sinner He giveth travail, to gather and to heap up that He may give to him that is good before God"

(Ecclesiastes 2:26). Ecclesiastes 3:1 also talks about seasons, time, and purpose for everything. Wisdom will teach you when to speak, when to be quiet, when to act, and when to react. Wisdom, knowledge, and understanding will take you far while walking out your destiny and divine purpose on earth.

You should rely on wisdom to know when to speak or listen. I can attest that listening and hearing God when praying guarantees a fruitful prayer life.

---

1. "Intercession," dictionary.com, accessed September 7, 2018, https://www.dictionary.com/browse/intercession?s=t.
2. "Intervene," dictionary.com, accessed September 7, 2018, https://www.dictionary.com/browse/intervene?s=t.
3. "Intercede," dictionary.com, accessed September 7, 2018, https://www.dictionary.com/browse/intercede?s=t.
4. "Intercessor," dictionary.com, accessed September 7, 2018, https://www.dictionary.com/browse/intercessor?s=t.

Chapter Four: Who Can Become an Intercessor and the Character of an Intercessor?

Anyone can take part in intercessory prayer, but not all are called to be intercessors or raised up as such. Many scriptures in God's Word address who God called into position based on their purpose, according to His will. I have discovered that intercessors usually know if they have been called to this position. Some just naturally pray for others and stand in the gap for them. Intercessors face many risks and sacrifices. This call is not to be taken lightly.

A very common trait of an intercessor is the willingness to volunteer to pray for people without being asked to pray. They also pray for those who come to mind and who are placed on their heart, regardless of the time of day or night. Many nights, I am awakened with a person's face in front of me, or I hear their name in the spirit, and I pray as the Holy Spirit leads, sometimes for hours. At other times, I am praying throughout the night. This can and has gone on for days and nights, involving many sleepless nights. But God sustained me so that I could get up the next day and function at a full-time job. Through the strength of Christ, I endure and press on to do God's will. I am sure other intercessors reading the book will agree. "We can do all things through Christ who strengthens us" (Philippians 4:13).

Intercessors' hearts are turned toward standing in the gap for others and are usually very passionate and compassionate toward others. The key word is heart. A heart-to-heart connection with God is fundamental if you want any type of relationship with Him and to have a successful ministry. I believe as an intercessor, you must have a heart for people, and, most of all, you must be a person after the heart of God. What is in your heart is what will come out of your mouth. Luke 6:45b says, "For of the abundance of the heart, His mouth speaketh."

Another trait of an intercessor is a willingness to do something. Someone who volunteers is not necessarily someone who is asked, but rather someone who steps forward to accomplish something, no matter the situation, the level of involvement, or the outcome. In John 15:13, Jesus said, "Greater love hath no man than this, that a man lay down His life for His friends." A true intercessor *takes risks and sacrifices themselves* for others, no matter the cost.

For instance, David, one of my favorite intercessors, reveals this in the scripture in 1 Samuel. When he was a young boy, he was willing to face death from Goliath for the sake of Israel. He was interceding for others at the risk of his own life. If death was not on his heart for Israel's sake, he was at least willing to face humiliation, failure, and defeat with Goliath. In this story about David in the scripture, you can see David's willingness to take a risk, which was within him as a child. It was a part of his nature and more importantly, he knew that God was with him, because he had established an intimate relationship with God at an early age. We must know that God is with us when interceding for others, and He will not allow any weapon formed against us to prosper. (See Isaiah 54:17)

The Story of David and Goliath (1 Samuel 17)

Now the Philistines gathered together their armies to battle, and were gathered together at Shochoh, which belongeth to Judah, and pitched between Shochoh and Azekah, in Ephesdammim. And Saul and the men of Israel were gathered together, and pitched by the valley of Elah, and set the battle in array against the Philistines. And the Philistines stood on a mountain on the one side, and Israel stood on a mountain on the other side: and there was a valley between them.

And there went out a champion out of the camp of the Philistines, named Goliath, of Gath, whose height was six cubits and a span. And he had a helmet of brass upon his head, and he was armed with a coat of mail; and the weight of the coat was five thousand shekels of brass. And he had greaves of brass upon his legs and a target of brass between his shoulders. And the staff of his spear was like a weaver's beam; and his spear's head weighed six hundred shekels of iron: and one bearing a shield went before him.

And he stood and cried unto the armies of Israel, and said unto them, "Why are ye come out to set your battle in array? Am not I a Philistine, and ye servants to Saul? Choose you a man for you, and let him come down to me. If he be able to fight with me, and to kill me, then will we be your servants: but if I prevail against him, and kill him, then shall ye be our servants, and serve us." And the Philistine said, "I defy the armies of Israel this day; give me a man, that we may fight together."

When Saul and all Israel heard those words of the Philistine, they were dismayed, and greatly afraid.

Now David was the son of that Ephrathite of Bethlehemjudah, whose name was Jesse; and he had eight sons: and the man went among men for an old man in the days of Saul. And the three eldest sons of Jesse went and followed Saul to the battle: and the names of his three sons that went to the battle were Eliab the firstborn, and next unto him Abinadab, and the third Shammah. And David was the youngest: and the three eldest followed Saul. But David went and returned from Saul to feed his father's sheep at Bethlehem. And the Philistine drew near morning and evening, and presented himself forty days.

And Jesse said unto David his son, "Take now for thy brethren an ephah of this parched corn, and these ten loaves, and run to the camp of thy brethren; and carry these ten cheeses unto the captain of their thousand, and look how thy brethren fare, and take their pledge."

Now Saul, and they, and all the men of Israel, were in the valley of Elah, fighting with the Philistines. And David rose up early in the morning, and left the sheep with a keeper, and took, and went, as Jesse had commanded him; and he came to the trench, as the host was going forth to the fight, and shouted for the battle. For Israel and the Philistines had put the battle in array, army against army. And David left his carriage in the hand of the keeper of the carriage, and ran into the army, and came and saluted his brethren. And as he talked with them, behold, there came up the champion, the Philistine of Gath, Goliath by name, out of the armies of the Philistines, and spake according to the same words: and

David heard them. And all the men of Israel, when they saw the man, fled from him, and were sore afraid.

And the men of Israel said, "Have ye seen this man that is come up? Surely to defy Israel is he come up: and it shall be that the man who killeth him, the king will enrich him with great riches, and will give him his daughter, and make his father's house free in Israel."

And David spake to the men that stood by him, saying, What shall be done to the man that killeth this Philistine, and taketh away the reproach from Israel? for who is this uncircumcised Philistine, that he should defy the armies of the living God?"

And the people answered him after this manner, saying, "So shall it be done to the man that killeth him."

And Eliab his eldest brother heard when he spake unto the men; and Eliab's anger was kindled against David, and he said, "Why camest thou down hither? And with whom hast thou left those few sheep in the wilderness? I know thy pride, and the naughtiness of thine heart; for thou art come down that thou mightest see the battle."

And David said, "What have I now done? Is there not a cause?" And he turned from him toward another and spake after the same manner: and the people answered him again after the former manner. And when the words were heard which David spake, they rehearsed them before Saul: and he sent for him. And David said to Saul, "Let no man's heart fail because of him; thy servant will go and fight with this Philistine."

And Saul said to David, "Thou art not able to go against this Philistine to fight with him: for thou art but a youth, and he a man of war from his youth."

And David said unto Saul, "Thy servant kept his father's

sheep, and there came a lion, and a bear, and took a lamb out of the flock: and I went out after him, and smote him, and delivered it out of his mouth: and when he arose against me, I caught him by his beard, and smote him, and slew him. Thy servant slew both the lion and the bear: and this uncircumcised Philistine shall be as one of them, seeing he hath defied the armies of the living God." David said moreover, "The Lord that delivered me out of the paw of the lion, and out of the paw of the bear, he will deliver me out of the hand of this Philistine."

And Saul said unto David, "Go, and the Lord be with thee." And Saul armed David with his armor, and he put a helmet of brass upon his head; also he armed him with a coat of mail.

And David girded his sword upon his armour, and he assayed to go; for he had not proved it. And David said unto Saul, "I cannot go with these; for I have not proved them." And David put them off him. And he took his staff in his hand, and chose him five smooth stones out of the brook, and put them in a shepherd's bag which he had, even in a scrip; and his sling was in his hand: and he drew near to the Philistine.

And the Philistine came on and drew near unto David; and the man that bare the shield went before him. And when the Philistine looked about, and saw David, he disdained him: for he was but a youth, and ruddy, and of a fair countenance. And the Philistine said unto David, "Am I a dog that thou comest to me with staves?" And the Philistine cursed David by his gods. And the Philistine said to David, "Come to me, and I will give thy flesh unto the fowls of the air, and to the beasts of the field."

Then said David to the Philistine, "Thou comest to me

with a sword, and with a spear, and with a shield: but I come to thee in the name of the Lord of hosts, the God of the armies of Israel, whom thou hast defied. This day will the Lord deliver thee into mine hand; and I will smite thee, and take thine head from thee; and I will give the carcases of the host of the Philistines this day unto the fowls of the air, and to the wild beasts of the earth; that all the earth may know that there is a God in Israel. And all this assembly shall know that the Lord saveth not with sword and spear: for the battle is the Lord's, and he will give you into our hands."

And it came to pass, when the Philistine arose, and came, and drew nigh to meet David that David hastened, and ran toward the army to meet the Philistine. And David put his hand in his bag, and took thence a stone and slang it, and smote the Philistine in his forehead, that the stone sunk into his forehead; and he fell upon his face to the earth. So David prevailed over the Philistine with a sling and with a stone, and smote the Philistine, and slew him; but there was no sword in the hand of David. Therefore David ran, and stood upon the Philistine, and took his sword, and drew it out of the sheath thereof, and slew him, and cut off his head therewith. And when the Philistines saw their champion was dead, they fled.

And the men of Israel and of Judah arose, and shouted, and pursued the Philistines, until thou come to the valley, and to the gates of Ekron. And the wounded of the Philistines fell down by the way to Shaaraim, even unto Gath, and unto Ekron. And the children of Israel returned from chasing after the Philistines, and they spoiled their tents. And David took the head of the Philistine, and brought it to Jerusalem; but he put his armour in his tent.

And when Saul saw David go forth against the Philistine, he said unto Abner, the captain of the host, "Abner, whose son is this youth?"

And Abner said, "As thy soul liveth, O king, I cannot tell."

And the king said, "Enquire thou whose son the stripling is."

And as David returned from the slaughter of the Philistine, Abner took him, and brought him before Saul with the head of the Philistine in his hand. And Saul said to him, "Whose son art thou, thou young man?"

And David answered, I am the son of thy servant Jesse the Bethlehemite.

This Bible story about David tells us a lot about his character. You might want to evaluate your character to see whether you are an intercessor if you are uncertain you have been called. You might also want to take it a step further and go before God, seek His face and ask Him to reveal any traits you must acquire to help determine if you are an intercessor. This was one of the first steps I took.

This book is to reveal our calling as intercessors and prayer warriors, but the most important revelation I hope everyone receives after reading this book is the understanding that praying should be a normal part of life for all of us, not just for intercessors. We all are commanded to pray for one another always.

Chapter Five: The Greatest Intercessor Who Walked the Earth

I want to talk about the greatest intercessor, Jesus who walked the earth who gives us the opportunity to have an intimate relationship with God, our Father. It begins through accepting Jesus Christ as our Savior and should elevate as we grow and develop in our walk with God. Jesus also provided us with examples of how to handle earthly situations: *Jesus Christ, our Lord and Savior.* The Bible tells us that he was born, crucified, died, and resurrected from the dead so that we can have eternal life. He intercedes on our behalf, according to Hebrews 7:25, which mentions that "He is able also to save them to the uttermost that come unto God by Him, seeing He ever liveth to make intercession for them." What an amazing gift and huge sacrifice! If we look at the great sacrifice He made for us, we should not hesitate to sacrifice ourselves to stand in the gap and intercede for others. He also gave us an example of praying for one another while giving up His life on the behalf of all who are unworthy of His sacrifice in Matthew 6, the Lord's Prayer.

This prayer shows Jesus's heart for others. He asks God for the needs of others, referenced in the verse that mentions our daily bread. He does not use the word *my* but says *our*, which means that we are included here. He asks God to forgive us of our sins and to deliver us from evil. This is a great example that shows us how we should pray for one another.

Jesus looked outside of Himself and His own concerns to see life from other's perspectives and prayed on their behalf. He was aware and vulnerable to the needs of others and prayed for them, which is substantial when interceding for others. We somehow have lost that in the woes of the world. It is time for us to come back to our purpose, praying for one another, encouraging one another, and living according to God's will.

I will not say it will be easy because it will not, but we must be committed to the purpose, plan, and vision of God and carry it out in these perilous times. Even as believers, we have forsaken others and mostly been focused on ourselves. And now look where we are! Listen to the world's woes. We need prayer, godly people! Prayer changes situations. I know this first hand. I have been obedient to do what God has commissioned me to do.

Those of us who are Christians know that Jesus is the Son of God, the bearer, bringer, and administrator of God's love. What God is—invisible in heaven—Jesus demonstrated as visible on earth. As mentioned earlier, Jesus came, lived, suffered, and died to glorify our Heavenly Father to let the world know how glorious the Father's love is toward us. What a powerful revelation! Many scriptures in the Bible demonstrate God's love for us and that Jesus is our intercessor. God's Word tells us that God wants to bless us and wants us to be joyful, happy. When reading the Bible with revelation and understanding, we should be able to comprehend that when we pray, God wants to bless us and that He want us to be full of joy on this earth.

Let's understand that Jesus is our true model of an intercessor. He is at the right hand of God, the Father interceding on our behalf. Jesus took the place of the priests in the Old Testament who were pure. They went into the temple and repented for the sins committed by the people.

Jesus is pure and clean, and His blood washes away all our sins daily when we confess them to Him before the throne of grace.

First Timothy 2:5,6 states, "There is one God, and one mediator between God and men, the man Christ Jesus, who gave himself a ransom for all, to be testified in due time." Jesus Christ walked the earth, free from all sin.

Jesus, our Intercessor, brings our sinful nature and our righteous God together at "a place of His blood" where He sacrificed Himself for our sins. We are now able to approach God based on the blood of Jesus that was shed on the cross of Calvary for the remission and forgiveness of our sins. Because of the blood of Jesus, we can approach God *boldly* without timidity, shyness or cowardliness. Hebrews 4:16 mentions, "Let us therefore come boldly unto the throne of grace that we may obtain mercy, and find grace to help in time of need."

While Jesus was here on earth, he provided examples of how to be an intercessor. He healed those who were sick and broken hearted and cast out demons from those who were possessed. He prayed for His disciples and even prayed for you and me when He interceded for all those who would believe in Him. But His intercession did not end when He ascended into heaven after His death and resurrection from the dead. He now serves as our Intercessor in heaven!

I am hoping that by this point in the book, you understand and have a revelation of three things:

- the character of an intercessor
- the urgency of intercession or intercessory prayer
- the importance of praying and how our relationship with God fits into our daily lives, especially our prayer lives

Chapter Six: What Prayer Means in Relation to God

The root word of prayer is pray. The online definition says to offer (a prayer). It is considered entering into spiritual communion with God.[1] John 4:24 mentions "God is a Spirit, and they that worship Him must worship Him in spirit and in truth".

I want to talk a little more about worship so that we can see the connection of *prayer with worship*. Psalm 96:9 says, "O Worship the Lord in the beauty of holiness: fear before Him, all the earth." The Hebrew word *barak* describes worship and means to kneel or bow, to give reverence to God as an act of adoration, implies a continual, conscious giving praise to God, to be attuned to Him and His presence.[2] The Hebrew word *shuwr* means strolling as a minstrel, to sing.[3]

Here's another main point of worship that has stuck with me. The following word most accurately describes praying and communicating with God. *Caphar*, which means to score with a mark, speak, talk, tell.[4] When we are praying to God, we are *speaking* to Him, *talking* with Him and *telling* Him what concerns us and; or affirming the solution according to His Word.

The Hebrew word for prayer, *tephillah* (תפלה), comes from the verb *palal* (פלל), which means intercession, supplication; by implication, a hymn.[5]

Another meaning of prayer is to make an earnest request to God.[6] Elias (Elijah) did exactly this, and God answered. This scripture lines up with the definition of the word pray(er), which is the act or practice of praying to God or an object of *worship*.

James 5:17–18 tells us that "Elias was a man subject to like passions as we are, and he prayed *earnestly* that it might not rain: and it rained not on the earth by the space of three years and six months. And he prayed again, and the heaven gave rain, and the earth brought forth her fruit" (emphasis added).

Pray(er) is the act of praying. Earlier, we established that prayer is one of the principle categories of worship. Therefore, prayer should always be our first choice or resource in any and all given situations. This is pleasing to God.

Prayer is simply talking with our Heavenly Father, our God. The Person who knows us better than we know ourselves, and who loves us more than anyone else does. We can talk with Him openly and honestly about anything with assurance that all will be well.

God is a being, a spiritual being, one who exists. We must reach a point of seeing Him as one who exists. He cannot be seen with the naked eye. I believe once we get to this place in our walk with God, we can know Him and be personal with Him in the same way that we are personal with those that we do see with our naked eye: our family, friends, church members, coworkers, business partners, and others.

When we want to get to know a person, the only way to do this is by spending time with them. It is the same with our Heavenly Father. We can easily tell Him what is on our mind, including our worries, pain, fear, hope, and joy. We can tell Him everything! Nothing is too big or too small to share with our God! He already knows. He is just waiting on us to share from our hearts.

Remember, God is God, but He is also a loving and caring Father who wants to hear our prayers and to know what is on the heart of His children. We need to learn to be ourselves with God. We should speak freely to Him without thinking that we need to talk a certain way. Just talk the way you would talk to anyone you have a close relationship with and you care about. Be transparent.

When you pray, position yourself to be attentive so that you can hear what God has to say to you. The communication should not be one-sided. Listening to God requires more patience and more practice than talking to Him.

God also speaks to us through the Bible. Listening to God is another way we can receive guidance as we seek His will. We can make sure that God is speaking because what we hear should *always* line up with God's Word. God never contradicts Himself in His Word.

When we pray, we come into the presence of God with a spirit-to-spirit connection. We are in the presence of the King of the earth, our Lord, and the Creator of everything. Prayer actually brings us into the throne room of God's grace.

Would you agree that this is where we make our supplications, requests, petitions, confessions, and praise known unto God? I believe whatever you want to say to God through communication based on His Word occurs in the throne room.

1. "Pray," dictionary.com, accessed September 7, 2018, https://www.dictionary.com/browse/pray?s=t.
2. "Hebrew Worship Words," justworship.com, accessed September 7, 2018, http://justworship.com/hebrew-words/.
3. Ibid
4. "H5608. Caphar," bibletools.org, accessed September 7, 2018, https://www.bibletools.org/index.cfm/fuseaction/Lexicon.show/ID/H5608/caphar.htm.
5. "8605," biblehub.com, accessed September 7, 2018, https://biblehub.com/str/hebrew/8605.htm.
6. "Prayer," vocabulary.com, accessed September 7, 2018, https://www.vocabulary.com/dictionary/prayer.

Chapter Seven: Change Your Prayer Life by Understanding the Order of Prayer

G od's Word was written *for* us, not *to* us. For years, I would not read my Bible as I should. I just talked to God all the time. I depended upon the pastor to read it for me and summarize the scriptures each Sunday. But the Word was written for my benefit, and it was my responsibility to gain wisdom, understanding, and revelation for myself. I soon discovered that I was out of balance. I found that the Bible is full of mysteries, and a relationship with God is crucial to understanding and receiving revelation of these mysteries. Proverbs 4:7 is one of my favorite passages and a profound scripture. It says, "Wisdom is the principle thing; therefore get wisdom: and with all thy getting get understanding."

God is very clever. He made sure that the Bible was written with deep mysteries only revealed through the Holy Spirit. As our relationship with God becomes deeper and as we move into an increased understanding of the Trinity (the

Father, Son and the Holy Spirit) in their fullness, the revelator begins to expose the hidden secrets in the Bible.

Most people I talk to are unaware of an order when praying before the Lord. First Timothy talks about the order of prayer and specifically mentions prayer in parts for a reason. After much studying, meditation, and seeking God's face about this book in the Bible, the revelation came, and the light bulb went on. First Timothy 2:1 says, *"First* of all, supplications, prayers, intercessions, and giving of thanks, be made for all men" (emphasis added). We must first entreat (humbly ask) God when going before Him in prayer.

We have talked about supplication in prior chapters, but we must include it in this chapter as well, since we are discussing order when praying to God.

Supplication means an act of supplicating, humble prayer, entreaty, or petition. Repentance comes through supplication, and forgiveness comes forth through repentance. You can always pray Psalm 51, which is known as a prayer of repentance. Acts 2:38–39 is significant in relation to repentance because it talks about what happens as a result of being baptized and receiving remission of our sins. Peter said unto them, *"Repent,* and *be baptized* every one of you in the name of Jesus Christ for the *remission of sins,* and *ye shall receive the gift* of the Holy Ghost. For *the promise (Holy Ghost) is unto you,* and to your children, and to all that are afar off" (emphasis added).

When praying for a group of people, we can pray according to Exodus 34:6–9. *"And the LORD passed by before Him, and proclaimed, The LORD, The LORD God, merciful and gracious, long-suffering, and abundant in goodness and truth, keeping mercy for thousands; forgiving iniquity and transgression and sin, and that will by no means clear the guilty; visiting the iniq-*

uity of the fathers upon the children, and upon the children's chil-
dren, unto the third and to the fourth generation. And Moses made
haste, and bowed His head toward the earth, and worshipped and I
say If now I have found grace in thy sight, as Moses did, O Lord, let
my Lord, I pray thee, go among us; for it is a stiffnecked people; and
pardon our iniquity and our sin, and take us for thine inheritance in
Jesus's name Amen.

God hears our cry when we go before Him in prayer with a broken heart and a contrite spirit, free from sin. We must connect with Him in spirit and in truth which also allows us to have a fruitful prayer life!

Psalm 51:10 tells us to allow God to create a clean heart and renew a steadfast spirit within us. We must render or surrender our heart (our inward man unto God *daily*. God hears our heartfelt prayers through sincere supplication.

First Timothy 2:1 mentions *petitions*, which are also prayer requests. Petition means a formally drawn request to a person in authority; soliciting some favor, right, mercy or other benefit. First Timothy 2:1 mentions *intercessions*, as the third part of prayer order, which I discussed in chapter 3, 2nd paragraph. Here, I will add that we are interceding for those we are led to pray for by the instructions of the Holy Spirit.

The last part of First Timothy 2:1 mentions *thanksgiving*, which is giving God thanks or to acknowledge how good He is to us and how much He loves us because we know He will be with us through the trials. *Victory* is ours. We give thanks and praise Him for what we believe He has already done for us through faith as we have prayed to Him. We give thanks because we love and need Him in our lives. We know by faith God hears us and will answer. We give thanks for the manifestation of what is already in the spiritual realm, waiting to manifest in the natural realm. Our God is not a God who would lie. He shall answer according to the purpose and plan He has for each of us corresponding to His will. Keep the faith!

Allow your flesh to be abased. Anxiety is an emotion; emotions are of the flesh. Emotions should not be present. We must surrender our soul and body unto the Lord and not be anxious about anything. We should allow our spirit man to rise to the occasion and enter into the presence of God with prayer; supplications, petitions, intercessions and thanksgiving.

When we are going through trials, our first response should be to go before God free from sin. There is not one issue or circumstance that we face on earth that the Bible does not provide a solution for. The Bible is our weapon against the wiles of the world.

At this point, we can stop reading for a few minutes and do this exercise: Lift up someone in prayer who has a need, concern, or difficult situation they are facing. As part of this exercise, we can also think of someone who needs healing and pray the following prayer.

Prayer for Healing

Feel free to add the name of the person or persons you are praying on behalf of where the word "me" is mentioned.

God, you sent Your Word, Jesus, and healed them and delivered them from their destructions. I know you will do the same for _____ (person's name) because it is truth.

(See Psalm 107:20.)

"I bless You LORD, O my soul; and all that is within me, I bless your holy name! I Bless You LORD, O my soul, and forget not all your benefits: Who forgives all my iniquities, who heals all my

diseases, who redeems my life from destruction, who crowns me with lovingkindness and tender mercies" (Psalm 103:1–4, NKJV).

"Jesus was wounded for my transgressions, He was bruised for my iniquities: the chastisement of my peace was upon Him; and with His stripes I am healed" (Isaiah 53:5) In Jesus's name.

"O LORD my God, I have cried unto thee and thou hast healed me" (Psalm 30:2). Thank you, Lord God, for your healing virtue In Jesus's Name. Amen

First Samuel 12:23 says, "Moreover as for me, *God forbid that I should sin against the Lord in ceasing to pray for you,* but I will teach you the good and the right way" (emphasis added). This scripture proves the importance of interceding for others, which is an integral part of prayer. We should learn to be diligent in praying for one another. This scripture also indicates that we are sinning against God if we stop praying for one another, which was an eye-opening revelation to me when I read and meditated on the passage years ago while in training to become an intercessor.

Chapter Eight: Reasons to Seek God's Face during Prayer

W e must understand the grace and mercy of God. A crucial component to prayer is seeking God's face. How we approach God during prayer could hugely impact the results we receive. This was a powerful revelation for me. We should seek God's face when going before the throne of grace and the mercy seat of God. His mercy is essential when praying to Him.

We *seek* God's mercy when we pray to Him because we can do nothing to change our situation; we cannot even always change a situation by prayer. If we could, we can all think of numerous times that we have prayed for something, but it just did not turn out the way we expected. Psalm 145:9 says, "The Lord is good to all: and His tender mercies are over all His works." God's mercy is over the situation.

This verse means that all He does for us involves His mercy upon us and on the situation at hand. Romans 9:16 tells us, "So then it is not of him that willeth; nor of him

that runneth, *but of God that sheweth mercy*." This scripture
refers to us. We do not will nor do we run anything in our
lives, whether or not we want to acknowledge it. This state-
ment is *not* my opinion but truth according to the Word of
God. (Romans 9:16, emphasis added).

David always went before God, seeking His face in
prayer, crying out for God's mercy when in need. David
was a man after the heart of God and is considered, in my
opinion, a true intercessor who received answers to His
prayers. I will talk about others later, but I want to tie
David in with God's mercy in hopes of better understanding and receiving revelation of God's mercy in times
of need.

Second Samuel 24:14 mentions that David said unto
God, "I am in a great strait: let us fall now into the hand of
the LORD; for His mercies are great: and let me not fall into
the hand of man."

Psalm 86:5 says, "For thou, Lord, art good, and ready to
forgive; and plenteous in mercy unto all them that call upon
thee."

Prayer is pleasing to God and should be intimate
communication with God. As a refresher, the word intimate
means private or closely personal. This type of intimacy can
only occur in your secret place where you are seeking God's
face, encountering His presence and having an intimate and
personal experience with God. Not only do we need His
help, but our lives are driven by His goodness and mercy. I
will go as far as to say that I believe His mercy in our lives
could depend upon how relational we are with Him. It is all
about God and His mercy.

The Greek word for mercy is *eleos*, which means mercy,
pity, and compassion.[1] Strong's concordance defines the

chief Hebrew word for mercy, *chesed*, as goodness, kindness, faithfulness.[2]

Are we truly always under God's covenant when we go before Him in prayer?

Psalm 23

(A psalm of David – emphasis added)
The Lord is my shepherd, I shall not want
He maketh me to lie down in green pastures;
He leadeth me beside the still waters,
He restoreth my soul
He leadeth me in the paths of righteousness
For His name's sake.
Yea though I walk through the valley of the shadow of death
I will fear no evil for thou art with me;
Thy rod and thy staff they comfort me.
Thou preparest a table before me in the presence of mine enemies;
Thou anointest my head with oil; my cup runneth over,
Surely goodness and mercy shall follow me all the days of my life;
And I will dwell in the house of the Lord forever.

In His presence, we have His goodness and mercy in our lives always, all the days of our lives.

Psalm 103:17 tells us that "the mercy of the Lord is from everlasting to everlasting upon them that fear Him, and the righteousness unto children's children."

He will lead, restore, prepare, and anoint us. We should always want to be in His presence when we are confronted with the things of this world. We know that He is with us and will have mercy upon every area of our lives and provide for us. We should know His grace is more than enough. Second Corinthians 12:9 says, "His grace is sufficient for us."

The Greek word *charis* means grace, favor, joy, pleasure, delight, loveliness and kindness.[3] Strong's concordance definition of grace is a gift or blessing brought to man by Jesus.[4] Over and over He tells us in His Word, "Know that I am God." We must truly know this and not waver, doubt, or fear.

All we need is the faith of a mustard seed, along with an open relationship with our God. I can testify that the stronger your prayer life becomes with our Father God, the more your faith builds, and the blessed assurance of His everlasting love becomes evident within your heart and in your life. The love, grace, and mercy of God are forevermore and never leave us.

We are saved by God's grace and mercy and by the acceptance of Jesus Christ, our Savior, and His blood washes our sins. Titus 3:5–7 states, "Not by works of righteousness which we have done, but according to His Mercy He saved us, by the washing of regeneration, and renewing of the Holy Ghost; which He shed on us abundantly through Jesus Christ our Saviour, That being justified by His Grace, we should be made heirs according to the hope of eternal life."

We should always be in worship with God, which will enhance our relationship with Him. Time spent in His presence will begin to affect us. We will become more like Him.

Seeking God's face and spending time in His presence praying transforms us and renews our mind within us. This has been my experience. The root word for transformation is transform, which means to change condition, nature, or character.[5] Romans 12:2 states, "not to be conformed to this world: but be ye *transformed* by the renewing of your mind, that ye may prove what is that good, and acceptable, and perfect, will of God" (emphasis added).

Remember that God calls His people to commune and communicate (worship) with Him, seek His face, stay in prayer, pray without ceasing, and stay connected with Him always. If we all follow this truth daily, our lives and the lives of others will all be better. I truly believe, with all my heart, that if we follow this one command, the world would not be in the state it is in today.

Prayer is very important in our lives and is our lifeline to God. I know I keep repeating some of the same statements, but as a former kindergarten teacher, I know that hearing the same thing over and over establishes that truth inside of us, which will not leave us. My aim in this book is to help you understand the importance of prayer so that you do not take it lightly. We always need prayer, whether we see life as grand or undesirable.

Our prayer life determines our outcome either way. Understanding our prayer life means communicating, spending time with, and *interacting with God* all the time.

Seeking God's face and praying keeps us on point to assure that we are always walking in righteousness, which keeps us in order and free from sinful acts, thus bringing about the betterment of mankind.

---

1. "Mercy," biblehub.com, accessed September 7, 2018, https://biblehub.com/greek/1656.htm.
2. "KJV & Strongs h2617," blueletterbible.org, accessed September 7, 2018, https://www.blueletterbible.org/lang/lexicon/lexicon.cfm?t=kjv&strongs=h2617.

3. "Charis," biblestudytools.com, accessed September 7, 2018, https://www.biblestudytools.com/lexicons/greek/nas/charis.html.

4. "Grace," biblehub.com, accessed September 7, 2018, https://biblehub.com/greek/5485.htm.

5. "Transform," dictionary.com, accessed September 7, 2018, https://www.dictionary.com/browse/transform?s=t.

Chapter Nine: Preparing Our Hearts and going Before God

W e must go before the Lord in *righteousness* and *purity*. Our spirit, not our flesh, connects with God. We cannot connect with God in the flesh but in *spirit and truth*. First Samuel 7:3 says, "Samuel spake unto all the house of Israel, saying, If ye do return unto the Lord with all your hearts, then put away the strange gods and Ashtaroth from among you, and *prepare your hearts* unto the Lord, and serve Him only: and He will deliver you out of the hand of the Philistines." Heart preparation for prayer is significant. Psalm 24:3–4 clearly tells us to prepare our hearts when going before the Lord.

A heart-to-heart relationship with God in prayer is very important. I cannot express this enough. If we understand the importance of this, we will receive revelation of how significant prayer is to God and to our daily walk as Christians and believers.

Our prayers should come from our hearts, full of *truth*, using our lips as our mouth piece to communicate or commune with God. The Hebrew definition of true (*emeth*) is faith, faithfulness, lasting, and sureness and was understood to be an attribute of God.[1]

We must prepare our hearts for fellowship with God. God searches the heart, and David asked God to search His heart in Psalm 139:23. Prayer is heartfelt. We should learn to pray in this manner when we are going before God in prayer.

Are your prayers heartfelt? Psalm tells us that both the heart and the spirit are *keys* to open the gateway of connecting with God in prayer. "The sacrifices of God are a broken spirit; a broken and a contrite heart" (Psalm 51:17).

Broken represents humility and submission. This is why I believe a heart of *humility* must be evident when going before the Lord. First Peter 5:5b–6 emphasizes our need for humility by repeating the command to humble ourselves. "Be subject one to another, and be clothed with humility; for God resisteth the proud, and giveth grace to the humble. *Humble yourselves* therefore under the mighty hand of God, that He may exalt you in due time." These scriptures show us the benefits of humility and the importance of having *a heart of humility* when walking with the Lord. Humility in the dictionary means the quality or condition of being humble.[2] Synonyms are lowliness, meekness, and submissiveness. When we are going before the throne of grace, the instructions here state to be clothed in humility.

We should also have a submissive mindset, prepared to submit ourselves unto the Lord. Submissive means yielding to authority of another; humbly obedient.[3]

We must also be willing to be convicted, convicted of our flaws in relation to our faith in Christ. As we understand that believing in God requires a yielding of our whole heart, life, and will, we will receive revelation that we should strive to be a humble person on this earth. Humility leads us to full faith in Christ so that each of us individually and corporately will receive the fullness of God in our lives. Ephesians 4:12–15 says, *"For the perfecting of the saints, for the work of the ministry, for the edifying of the body of Christ: Till we all come in the unity of the faith, and of the knowledge of the Son of God, unto a perfect man, unto the measure of the stature of the fullness of Christ: That we henceforth be no more children, tossed to and fro, and carried about with every wind of doctrine, by the sleight of men, and cunning craftiness, whereby they lie in wait to deceive; but speaking the truth in love, may grow up into Him in all things, which is the head, even Christ"* (emphasis added).

We must confess our sins, iniquities, and transgressions unto God and ask forgiveness [repent] so that when we go to our Heavenly Father in Jesus's name, the blood of Jesus cleanses us of our sins and prepares us to truly connect with God. The following scriptures about sin, iniquity, and transgression clarify this.

Sin is the act of violating God's will. The will of God for each of us as believers is described and outlined in the Bible and whenever we go against His commands, it is against God's will. We have sinned against God.

Iniquity is immoral behavior or any behavior that is unrighteous. If it is not something God condones or approves of based on what the Bible says, it is immoral behavior; therefore, it is iniquity.

Transgression is violating a command. Any command that God has given us to follow. If we violate that command, we have transgressed in God's eyes. Some people believe sin, iniquity, and transgression are all the same. Early on in my walk with Christ, I thought this as well until I started reading God's Word. I discovered they are all different, but all are not pleasing to God. Here are some scriptures in Isaiah that indicate *transgression, iniquity* and *sin* are not the same.

Isaiah 59:10–13 says, "we grope for the wall like the blind, and we grope as if we had no eyes: we stumble at noon day as in the night; we are in desolate places as dead men. We roar all like bears, and mourn sore like doves: we look for judgment, but there is none; for salvation, but it is far off from us. For our *transgressions* (violation of God's commands) are multiplied before thee, and our *sins* (violating or going against God's will) testify against us: for our transgressions are with us; and as for our *iniquities,* (immoral behaviors) we know them; In transgressing and lying iniquity against the Lord, and departing away from our God, speaking oppression and revolt, conceiving and uttering from the heart words of falsehood" (emphasis added).

We are forgiven because Jesus was forsaken, as it is written in Matthew 27:46, which was predestined so that we would have the opportunity to an open door of eternal life. Jesus felt abandoned. I consider this an ultimate example of God's amazing love for us.

Asking for forgiveness and being forgiven by God is a sign that we are pure of heart and clean from sin before going to God in prayer. We pray what is on our hearts unto Abba, Father. First John 3:21–22 says, "Beloved, if our heart condemns us not, then have we confidence toward God. And whatsoever we ask, we receive of Him, because we keep His commandments, and do those things that are pleasing in His sight."

We need to see ourselves dead to transgression, iniquity, and sin. Be sinless before the eyes of our Abba Father so that we are pleasing in His sight. We must also forgive all who have offended or hurt us. The Bible says in Mark 11:25–26, "When ye stand praying, forgive, if ye have ought against any: that our Father also which is in heaven may forgive our trespasses. But if we do not forgive, neither will our Father which is in heaven forgive our trespasses."

We must be aware that the forgiveness we seek from the Father comes after we have forgiven those who have asked our forgiveness and those who have not. We still must forgive them if we have offence toward them. Yes, we must forgive all those who have offended us.

Forgiveness is an action, not a hidden secret. It is probably the most difficult thing we are asked and required to do and it is not possible without God's direct intervention in us. Each day we come up short one way or the other. The thing we said we would never do, we find ourselves doing it again and again. Each time, God is willing to forgive us our sins; therefore, we *must* do the same with those who offend us.

What if the Lord treated us the way we treat others when they seek forgiveness? What if God turned His back on us the way we turn our back on others? Matthew 5:23–24 commands us, "If thou bring thy gift to the altar, and there rememberest that thy brother hath ought against thee; leave there thy gift before the altar, and go thy way; first be reconciled to thy brother, and then come and offer thy gift." Remember that going before God and seeking His face requires us to be free of sin. We must go before God with heartfelt worship. Prayer is a form of worship, and we must learn how to take time and prepare our hearts and our minds while praying and communing with God, creating a purpose in prayer. This purpose should reveal to us who we are in Christ Jesus. We know that we are more than conquerors.

Through prayer, God raises us up with His power by faith. When we ask in Jesus's name, we can move mountains and any obstacles we pray to be removed shall be removed according to God's will, and we will press on until the expected end manifests from the supernatural into the natural realm. Glory to God!

We *must believe* by faith, what we ask God according to His will shall come to pass in due season when we pray in Jesus's name. Mark 11:23 says, "Whosoever shall say unto this mountain, be thou removed, and be thou cast into the sea; and shall not doubt in his heart, but shall believe that those things which he saith shall come to pass; he shall have whatsoever he saith." Ecclesiastes 3:1 tells us "to everything there is a season and a time to every purpose under the heaven."

We also need to *have understanding of the Word* that relates to the solution of our need or request. Research the scriptures in the Bible that relate to the answer for the life challenge you are encountering and meditate on those scriptures. Have the scriptures ready to pray from your heart and pray the promises of God back to Him, reminding Him of His covenant with you. He will answer and help you. But you have a responsibility to God; to live according to His Word, and you must trust God that He will do what He said He would do for you according to His Word!

---

1. "Emeth," biblestudytools.com, accessed September 7, 2018, https://www.biblestudytools.com/lexicons/hebrew/nas/emeth.html.
2. "Humility," dictionary.com, accessed September 7, 2018, https://www.dictionary.com/browse/humility?s=t.
3. "Submissive," dictionary.com, accessed September 7, 2018, https://www.dictionary.com/browse/submissive?s=t.

Chapter Ten: Coming Before God (Holy Hands and a Pure Heart)

W e talked about preparing our hearts prior to going before the Lord in the previous chapter, which leads us into this chapter. Some of the material is repeated, but the reminders help the information stick with us. We must always seek after God with supplication, in sincerity.

You see, God is a God of order, and He gives us order throughout His Word. When we offer up our sins to God, asking Him to forgive us through Jesus Christ, our Intercessor washes us with His blood and makes us whiter than snow, according to Psalm 51:7.

As I have already said, we can only worship God in *spirit and truth*. When we enter God's presence, we must be free from sin, which we also previously discussed, so that we can have a *pure heart* and *holy hands*.

Confessing our sins unto God allows the blood to cleanse us and make us presentable to go before God. This assures us that we are pure at heart and cleansed from all sin. We know that we will be forgiven if our confession is sincere, spoken from our lips, and coming from our heart. This gives us the key to the door to enter into Abba Father's presence. We now have the privilege of supping with our Lord, which is pleasing in His sight.

We must prepare our hearts for repentance. Psalm 51 is a perfect prayer of supplication, which involves forgiveness and repentance before our Lord.

PRAYER OF SUPPLICATION
(Psalm 51)

"Have mercy upon me, O God, according to thy lovingkindness; according unto the multitude of thy tender mercies blot out my transgressions. Wash me thoroughly from mine iniquity, and cleanse me from my sin. For I acknowledge my transgressions: and my sin is ever before me. Against thee, thee only, have I sinned, and done this evil in thy sight: that thou mightest be justified when thou speakest, and be clear when thou judgest. Behold, I was shapen in iniquity; and in sin did my mother conceive me. Behold, thou desirest truth in the inward parts: and in the hidden part thou shalt make me to know wisdom. Purge me with hyssop, and I shall be clean: wash me, and I shall be whiter than snow. Make me to hear joy and gladness; that the bones which thou hast broken may rejoice. Hide thy face from my sins, and blot out all mine iniquities. Create in me a clean heart, O God; and renew a right spirit within me. Cast me not away from thy presence; and take not thy holy spirit from me. Restore unto me the joy of thy salvation; and uphold me with thy free spirit. Then will I teach transgressors thy ways; and sinners shall be converted unto thee. Deliver me from bloodguiltiness, O God, thou God of my salvation: and my tongue shall sing aloud of thy righteousness. O Lord, open thou my lips; and my mouth shall shew forth thy praise. For thou desirest not sacrifice; else would I give it: thou delightest not in burnt offering.

The sacrifices of God are a broken spirit: a broken and a contrite heart, O God, thou wilt not despise." In Jesus Name. Amen

Remember, our Heavenly Father does not condone or approve of sin, and we must always be sin free (repented and asked for forgiveness) when we go before Him with our prayer needs.

Chapter Eleven: Praying the Solution Instead of the Problem

Y ou might be asking yourself what I mean by this. Some of you may know exactly what I mean. At one point in my life, I would not have known what this meant either. We have all been there at some point. On my part, I had a lack of understanding and a lack of teaching as I did not receive much instruction on this subject in my early walk with God.

For many years, I thought the way to pray to God was by telling Him what I needed and what was wrong. My lack of reading the Bible with understanding contributed to this issue, and more importantly, I did not know who God was to me. God's Word is full of solutions *not* problems. I soon became aware that God was not hearing me. His Word says to ask in His name and it will be done, but He also says in Matthew 6:7–8, "When ye pray, use not vain repetitions as the heathen do. For they think that they will be heard for their much speaking. Be not ye therefore like unto them. For your Father knoweth what things ye have need of before ye ask Him." This passage cannot be any clearer. Jesus says that the Father knows the things we need before we ask Him. This was so profound! Why are we praying our needs, concerns, and desires as opposed to praying *His promises—the answers to the needs and desires?*

Remember that we should not be concerned with praying our problems to God; He already knows them. We should be concerned with reading the solution in His Word, meditating and praying the Word, which are His promises to us, back to Him.

We should remind God of His promises and His covenant with us through faith, believing the expected end shall come to pass in due season. Give God the glory due His name for answering prayers. He is a God of answered prayers!

If you are a new Christian or believer reading this book, you can always pray the Lord's Prayer. Matthew 6 tells us that He knows what we need, and you can pray this prayer, and be assured that He is listening. I believe everything troubling us when praying this prayer God will answer.

The Lord's Prayer
(Matthew 6:9–14)

Our Father in heaven,
Hallowed be your name.
Your kingdom come.
Your will be done
On earth as it is in heaven.
Give us (me) this day our (my) daily bread.
And forgive us (me) our (my) debts,
As we (I) forgive our (my) debtors.

And do not lead us (me) into temptation,
But deliver us (me) from the evil one.
For yours (mine) is the kingdom and the power and the glory forever.
Amen.

You can pray the Lord's Prayer daily, and you will be comforted in every area of life circumstances. I received revelation of this powerful prayer. The Lord's Prayer is a prayer of *humility* and of *submission, releasing our will* to the Father. We are giving Him control of our daily walk. (Your will be done.) In order for this to happen, we must be sensitive to His voice and know it. We are asking God to give us or provide for us what we need to function in the world and remain righteous in our daily walk. This prayer acknowledges that God *sustains* and *provides* for us as *Jehovah Jireh*. He is our provider. We cannot walk a righteous life without the bread from heaven.

This bread also represents our *spiritual nourishment* received (manna from heaven) to be healthy in the spirit of righteousness. We eat bread or food to be healthy in the natural. We exercise by walking, running, and working out. We will become weak if we do not eat properly and even worse, we can become very ill. If we compare the natural need for bread or nourishment to the spiritual need (reading God's Word), we will see the symbolism of Christians needing daily spiritual bread to remain healthy spiritually!

The Lord's Prayer also relates to *repentance to the Father*, admitting our sins and *asking for forgiveness* and also at the same time, *expressing our forgiveness toward others* who have sinned against us. It is also a prayer of *protection*, asking the

Father to lead us not into temptation and to deliver us from anything or anyone that will bring harm upon us. (Emphasis added).

Keep these points in your mind and in your heart when you pray this prayer so that you can receive the fullness of what God intended when He gave Jesus permission to demonstrate this model prayer for guidance.

Chapter Twelve: Faith and Answers to Prayer

M any people believe that prayers are answered through repetition: praying the same prayer over and over or that the action of repeating the same thing over and over causes God to hear and answer. It should be our faith and works (action) why we believe that God will answer us. In my experience, listening and obeying when going before Him in prayer has been important to my receiving answered prayers.

When praying, take time to hear God speak and listen for the instructions (actions) you need to take to lead you toward the answer. When you pray, you should know in your heart, God will hear and answer your prayer because *faith without works (action) is dead."* James 2:17–26 tells us, "Even so faith, if it hath not works, is dead, being alone. Yea, a man may say, Thou hast faith, and I have works: shew me thy faith without thy works, and I will shew thee my faith by my works. Thou believest that there is one God; thou doest well: the devils also believe, and tremble. But wilt thou know, O vain man, that faith without works is dead? Was not Abraham our father justified by works, when he had offered Isaac his son upon the altar? Seest thou how faith wrought with his works, and by works was faith made perfect? And the scripture was fulfilled which saith, Abraham believed God, and it was imputed unto him for righteousness: and he was called the Friend of God. Ye see then how that by works a man is justified, and not by faith only. Likewise also was not Rahab the harlot justified by works, (actions) when she had received the messengers, and had sent them out another way; for as the body without the spirit is dead, so faith without works is dead also." Read all of James 2 for further insight.

As part of our *prayer* and *fellowship* time with God, we need to sustain our faith and be trained in hearing God's voice and obeying His commands. John 10:27 reads, "My sheep hear my voice, and I know them, and they follow me."

If we believe God is really God (Love), by faith, we must believe that God hears our prayers and shall answer! For this reason, we pray in Jesus's name as written in John 14:13–14. "Whatsoever ye shall ask in my name, that will I do, that the Father may be glorified in the Son. If ye ask anything *in my name*, I will do it" (emphasis added). Mark 11:24 informs us, "what things soever ye desire, when ye pray, *believe* that ye receive them, and ye shall have them" (emphasis added).

Believe through faith that our God *will not* forsake us.

Chapter Thirteen: Some Provisions Require Fasting and Praying

F asting and praying allows us to deny ourselves and humbles us. Commissions us to live righteously and most of all depend upon God for our answer through prayer when we are in need.

Fasting and praying means so much in successfully fulfilling the ministry God has called upon your life. As a Christian or believer, we are obligated to pray; it is also our obligation to fast. Read Matthew 6:16 which substantiates we should fast. Jesus says in this scripture "when you fast" not "if you fast".

Prayer is so dynamic to all God wants to do in the earth and so important to us that sometimes we must deny ourselves both food and sleep. Matthew 17:14–21 tells the story of the man who brings his lunatic child vexed by demons before the Lord. Jesus tells the disciples casting out demons requires more than just praying. He clearly states in this scripture that the only way they could cast out demons is through fasting and praying. Some prayer requests require both of these for a breakthrough!

Recognizing and connecting with the Holy Spirit in our day-to-day journey will help us while revealing all things to us. Scripture tells us that the Holy Spirit is our helper. I always consult the Holy Spirit now when praying, but this was not always the case. I was not aware of the importance of the Holy Spirit during prayer or as a part of my life. Jesus gives us an example of praying through the night, denying himself of sleep. Luke 6:12 says, "It came to pass in those days, that He (Jesus) went out into a mountain to pray, and continued all night in prayer to God." We must sometimes lose sleep when called to pray.

God's Word is our lifeline, full of truth. If we follow God's Word, we will have the full measure of joy on this earth. I truly believe combined *fasting* and *prayer* is a part of experiencing the full measure of joy. The Holy Spirit will inform you when you should fast and pray. He always directs me.

Story of Ezra

Ezra 8:21–23 says, "I proclaimed a fast there, at the river of Ahava, that we might afflict ourselves before our God, to seek of Him a right way for us, and for our little ones, and for all our substance. For I was ashamed to require of the king a band of soldiers and horsemen to help us against the enemy in the way: because we had spoken unto the king, saying, The hand of our God is upon all them for good that seek Him; but His power and His wrath is against all them that forsake Him. So we fasted and besought our God for this: and He was intreated of us."

In this passage, you can see that after they fasted, prayed and sought after God, God intreated them. Sought after or *chanan* in Hebrew means to show mercy.[1] Intreated or *athar* in Hebrew means prayer answered.[2]

Story of Esther

Esther, one of my favorite books in the Bible, also reveals the importance of fasting and praying. This woman of God travails by seeking God on the matter and getting direction for how to handle the situation.

After seeking God, she passed along the instructions she received, which was to gather all the Jews and ask them to fast along with her and her maidens. Not only were they instructed to fast, but they were given a specific time frame. Esther 4:16–17 further explains this. "Go, gather together all the Jews that are present in Shushan, and fast ye for me, and neither eat nor drink *three* days, night or day: I also and my maidens will fast likewise; and so will I go in unto the king, which is not according to the law: and if I perish, I perish. So Mordecai went his way, and did according to all that Esther had commanded him." (Emphasis added).

Esther 5:1–5 goes on to say the king listened and did as Esther commanded. After Esther, the maidens, and the Jews obeyed the Lord, Esther received insight from God on how to handle the situation, even though the instructions seemed farfetched. Her actions warranted her favor in the King's sight. The word warranted means authorization, sanction, or justification.[3] Reading the book of Esther will give you more insight into Esther as an intercessor.

Story of Jehosaphat

Second Chronicles talks about Jehoshaphat who feared the Lord and set himself to seek the Lord and proclaim a fast throughout all Judah. They gathered themselves together to pray before the Lord for help in their time of trouble. God heard their prayers and the affirmation of His promises to them and appeared and answered them.

Second Chronicles 20:1–30 states, "It came to pass after this also, that the children of Moab, and the children of Ammon, and with them other beside the Ammonites, came against Jehoshaphat to battle. Then there came some that told Jehoshaphat, saying, There cometh a great multitude against thee from beyond the sea on this side Syria; and, behold, they be in Hazazontamar, which is Engedi. And Jehoshaphat feared, and set himself to seek the Lord, and proclaimed a fast throughout all Judah. And Judah gathered themselves together, to ask help of the Lord: even out of all the cities of Judah they came to seek the Lord. And Jehoshaphat stood in the congregation of Judah and Jerusalem, in the house of the Lord, before the new court, and said, O Lord God of our fathers, art not thou God in heaven? And rulest not thou over all the kingdoms of the heathen? And in thine hand is there not power and might, so that none is able to withstand thee? Art not thou our God, who didst drive out the inhabitants of this land before thy people Israel, and gavest it to the seed of Abraham thy friend forever? And they dwelt therein, and have built thee a sanctuary therein for thy name, saying, if, when evil cometh upon us, as the sword, judgment, or pestilence, or famine, we stand before this house, and in thy presence, (for thy name is in this house,) and cry unto thee in our affliction, then thou wilt hear and help. And now, behold, the children of Ammon and Moab and mount Seir, whom thou wouldest not let Israel invade, when they came out of the land of Egypt, but they turned from them, and destroyed them not; Behold, I say, how they reward us, to come to cast us out of thy possession, which thou hast given us to inherit. O our God, wilt thou not judge them? For we have no might against this great company that cometh against us; neither know we what to do: but our eyes are upon thee.

"And all Judah stood before the Lord, with their little ones, their wives, and their children. Then upon Jahaziel the son of Zechariah, the son of Benaiah, the son of Jeiel, the son of Mattaniah, a Levite of the sons of Asaph, came the Spirit of the Lord in the midst of the congregation; And he said, Hearken ye, all Judah, and ye inhabitants of Jerusalem, and thou king Jehoshaphat, Thus saith the Lord unto you, be not afraid nor dismayed by reason of this great multitude; for *the battle is not yours, but God's.* Tomorrow go ye down against them: behold, they come up by the cliff of Ziz; and ye shall find them at the end of the brook, before the wilderness of Jeruel. Ye shall not need to fight in this battle: set yourselves, stand ye still, and see the salvation of the Lord with you, O Judah and Jerusalem: fear not, nor be dismayed; tomorrow go out against them: for the Lord will be with you. And Jehoshaphat bowed his head with his face to the ground: and all Judah and the inhabitants of Jerusalem fell before the Lord, worshipping the Lord. And the Levites, of the children of the Kohathites, and of the children of the Korhites, stood up to praise the Lord God of Israel with a loud voice on high. And they rose early in the morning, and went forth into the wilderness of Tekoa: and as they went forth,

"Jehoshaphat stood and said, Hear me, Judah, and ye inhabitants of Jerusalem; *Believe in the Lord your God, so shall ye be established; believe His prophets, so shall ye prosper.* And when he had consulted with the people, *he appointed singers unto the Lord, and that should praise the beauty of holiness, as they went out before the army, and to say, Praise the Lord; for his mercy endureth forever.* And when they began to sing and to praise, the Lord set ambushments against the children of Ammon, Moab, and mount Seir, which were come against Judah; and they were smitten. For the children of Ammon and Moab stood up against the inhabitants of mount Seir, utterly to slay and destroy them: and when they had made an end of the inhabitants of Seir, every one helped to destroy another. And when Judah came toward the watch tower in the wilderness, they looked unto the multitude, and, behold, they were dead bodies fallen to the earth, and none escaped. And when Jehoshaphat and his people came to take away the spoil of them, they found among them in abundance both riches with the dead bodies, and precious jewels, which they stripped off for themselves, more than they could carry away: and they were three days in gathering of the spoil, it was so much.

"And on the fourth day they assembled themselves in the valley of Berachah; for there they blessed the Lord: therefore the name of the same place was called, the valley of Berachah, unto this day. Then they returned, every man of Judah and Jerusalem, and Jehoshaphat in the forefront of them, to go again to Jerusalem with joy; for the Lord had made them to rejoice over their enemies. And they came to Jerusalem with psalteries and harps and trumpets unto the house of the Lord. And the fear of God was on all the kingdoms of those countries, when they had heard that the Lord fought against the enemies of Israel. So the realm of Jehoshaphat was quiet: for his God gave him rest round about" (emphasis added).

Story of Anna

Book of Luke speaks of Anna, a prophetess that had gone before God with fasting and praying day and night. Sometimes you might need to fast and pray day and night to receive your answer from God, but the Holy Spirit directs your path. Just wait until you hear instructions from God and move forward accordingly.

Luke 2:36–38 tells us, "Anna, a prophetess, the daughter of Phanuel, of the tribe of Aser: she was of a great age, and had lived with an husband seven years from her virginity; And she was a widow of about fourscore and four years, which departed not from the temple, but *served God with fastings and prayers night and day.* And she coming in that instant gave thanks likewise unto the Lord, and spake of Him to all them that looked for redemption in Jerusalem" (emphasis added).

We do not want to get hung up on a ritual or mores (customs or traditions) when communicating with God because we can become legalistic. Instead we should stay open for newness or freshness in the Lord always! Lamentations 3:22–23 states, "It is of the Lord's mercies that we are not consumed, because His compassions fail not. They are new every morning: great is thy faithfulness." We can see from the above scripture that God is about newness.

God's Word tells us that fasting is important in developing a closer relationship with Him: giving your heart and surrendering unto the Lord and answering yes to His call and His ways.

Joel 2:12–13 further emphasizes this. "The Lord, says turn ye even to me with *all* your heart, and with *fasting,* and with weeping, and with mourning: And rend your heart, (inward man) and not your garments, (outward man) and turn unto the Lord your God: for He is gracious and merciful, slow to anger, and of great kindness, and repenteth him of the evil." (Emphasis added).

We must understand and have revelation of this when entering God's presence in prayer. No, God is not complicated, but He is a God of order and process. For a further example of this, see Genesis concerning the creation.

We should want to be in the presence of the Lord in prayer, according to His Word, to receive the benefits of His promises.

At times, I have been instructed by the Holy Spirit to fast. I would sometimes question the instructions because fasting is a sacrifice. Now that I have developed a genuine, intimate relationship with God, I no longer question Him when I am called to fast. I just obey because I know I will make it through. First Samuel 15:22 emphasizes the importance of obedience and how it is better than sacrifice.

When I need to hear specific and clear instructions, I fast and pray. When fasting, I know for sure that I have heard the voice of the Lord. I can then by faith move forward with the instructions from the Holy Spirit, believing God will allow me to prevail. Exodus 34:28 tells us that when Moses went before God for forty days and forty nights, he did not eat nor drink. As mentioned earlier, sometimes we must *fast* and *pray* to press through the situation!

I am compelled to share Matthew 17:15-21 and Joel 2:12

related to fasting and praying as they will provide the clarity that fasting is vital to prayer, especially if you are an intercessor or prayer warrior interceding on behalf of others.

Matthew 17:15–21 says, "Lord, have mercy on my son: for he is lunatick and sore vexed: for ofttimes he falleth into the fire, and oft into the water. And I brought him to thy disciples, and they could not cure him. Then Jesus answered and said, O faithless and perverse generation, how long shall I be with you? How long shall I suffer you? Bring him hither to me. And Jesus rebuked the devil; and he departed out of him: and the child was cured from that very hour. Then came the disciples to Jesus apart, and said, why could not we cast him out? And Jesus said unto them, Because of your unbelief: for verily I say unto you, if ye have faith as a grain of mustard seed, ye shall say unto this mountain, Remove hence to yonder place; and it shall remove; and nothing shall be impossible unto you. Howbeit kind goeth not out but by *prayer* and *fasting*" (emphasis added).

Joel 2:12 reads, "Therefore also now, saith the LORD, turn ye [even] to me with all your heart, and with *fasting*, and with weeping, and with mourning."

These scriptures represent a sacrifice or a result of fasting and praying, giving us examples that fasting and praying can be required in certain situations. As you seek God and wait for direction from the Holy Spirit to advise you of what prayer strategies you need for the situation at hand, God will make sure you hit a bull's eye when praying for yourself or others. Jesus said it best. Remember, *some situations require fasting and prayer.*

1. "Chanan," biblestudytools.com, accessed September 7, 2018, https://www.biblestudytools.com/lexicons/hebrew/kjv/chanan.html.
2. "Athar," biblestudytools.com, accessed September 7, 2018, https://www.biblestudytools.com/lexicons/hebrew/nas/athar.html.
3. "Warrant," dictionary.com, accessed September 7, 2018, https://www.dictionary.com/browse/warrant?s=t.

Chapter Fourteen: Effective Divine Prayer Life (EDPL)

Once again, an EDPL (effective divine prayer life) is also a result of having a genuine divine relationship with God, our Father; Jesus Christ, our Savior and Intercessor; and the Holy Spirit, our indwelling Helper, who sanctions us to live a fulfilling righteous life on earth.

We previously talked about the definition of intercession, but I wanted to reiterate it in this chapter. I want each person reading this to remember what you read and assure that revelation and understanding is released. Stop here to take time to evaluate your prayer life and determine if you pray effectively. Let's also pray this prayer together to shift to the next level.

Prayer to Elevate

Father God in the heavens, I lift up your name. Holy Spirit, release Your anointing in a special way upon each and every person reading this chapter. Permit them to receive revelation of your power, given to us as a promise and gift. We believe You, God, and only you, the true and living God who gave your only begotten Son so that we can have eternal life. Jesus, you are the living Word that walked the earth and ascended into heaven, leaving us with the gift and promise (the Holy Spirit) for those of us who believe by faith. We receive the fullness of the Holy Spirit's power dwelling within us and available to help us as we pray unto You, Father. I pray this and believe, by faith, that you will reveal yourself in a powerful way right now to each reader in Jesus's name. Amen.

It is easy to be discouraged when we pray, feeling as if our prayers are having no effect. One main point in praying is being aware that prayer is more than simply asking God to give us what we need, want, or desire.

Prayer is active and powerful communication with God, Jesus, and the Holy Spirit. It is also reading, meditating, and praying God's Word along with seeking the Lord, who is our Heavenly Father, and communing with Him!

I believe effective divine praying guarantees that God will answer us. If you doubt this, the most effective prayer I have ever prayed thus far is the prayer for my salvation, which God answered beyond all my expectations. Effective praying also results in the building of faith. It increases our assurance in God's Word. Some of you right now might be recalling past prayers to determine if you were effective when praying. Stop and take some time and assess your prayer life and have a few conversations with God while evaluating your method of praying to perceive if you have been praying effectively when praying to God.

Chapter Fifteen: Examples of Effective Prayers

When we pray, we expect results. In order to obtain results, we want to pray *effective strategic prayers*, which can be accomplished through persistent and consistent communication with Godhead (Trinity) meditating and reading and praying God's Word as previously mentioned.

The Bible gives us examples of effective answered prayers. As you read and meditate on them, you will see key notes that will impact your praying strategy. I have emphasized certain words that I believe are focal points in the passages. They impacted my prayer life, and I believe they will do the same for you and your prayer life.

God answered Moses's prayer when Moses asked Him not to destroy the Israelites. Yes, God repented (changed) His mind because of *God's relationship with Moses* and because of Moses's approach toward God. Exodus 32:11–13 says, "Moses besought the Lord His God, and said, Lord, why doth thy wrath wax hot against thy people, which thou hast brought forth out of the land of Egypt with great power, and with a mighty hand? Wherefore should the Egyptians speak, and say, for mischief did He bring them out, to slay them in the mountains, and to consume them from the face of the earth? Turn from thy fierce wrath, and repent of this evil against thy people. Remember Abraham, Isaac, and Israel, thy servants, to whom thou swarest by thine own self, and saidst unto them, I will multiply your seed as the stars of heaven, and all this land that I have spoken of will I give unto your seed, and they shall inherit it forever."

Elias's (Elijah's) Prayer Answered by God

James 5:17–18 shows us how Elias went before God, and God answered His prayers. The following scriptures relate that *Elias prayed earnestly before God*. Earnest means showing sincerity of feeling. "Elias was a man subject to like passions as we are, and he prayed earnestly that it might *not rain*: and it rained not on the earth by the space of three years and six months. After a long time, in the third year, Elias went before God and prayed again, but this time he *prayed for rain*. And he prayed again, and the heaven gave rain, and the earth brought forth her fruit" (emphasis added).

As you pray to God with a heart of sincerity and openness toward our Father about your feelings related to the situation, seek Him and read His Word for the solution. This will help you receive an answer to your prayer. God already knows our hearts. We should openly express how we truly feel and repent and ask for forgiveness, which paves the way to righteousness. This allows us to be free from sin, iniquity, or transgression so that we can commune with God. He will bend an ear to hear our cry and answer according to His perfect will. I am sure you will be blessed.

Hannah's Prayer Answered

First Samuel 2:1–4 explains to us, "Hannah prayed and said, my heart rejoiceth in the Lord, mine horn is exalted in the Lord; my mouth is enlarged over mine enemies; because I rejoice in thy salvation. There is none holy as the Lord; for there is none beside thee; neither is there any rock like our God. Talk no more so exceedingly proudly; let not arrogancy come out of your mouth: for the Lord is a God of knowledge, and by Him actions are weighed, the bows of the mighty men are broken, and they that stumbled are girded with strength."

In First Samuel 1:9–20, "Hannah rose up after they had eaten in Shiloh, and after they had drunk. Now Eli the priest sat upon a seat by a post of the temple of the Lord. And she was in bitterness of soul, and prayed unto the Lord, and wept sore. And she vowed a vow, and said, O Lord of hosts, if thou wilt indeed look on the affliction of thine handmaid, and remember me, and not forget thine handmaid, but wilt give unto thine handmaid a man child, then I will give him unto the Lord all the days of his life, and there shall no razor come upon his head. And it came to pass, as she continued praying before the Lord, that Eli marked her mouth. Now Hannah, she spake in her heart; only her lips moved, but her voice was not heard: therefore Eli thought she had been drunken. And Eli said unto her, How long wilt thou be drunken? Put away thy wine from thee. And Hannah answered and said, No, my lord, I am a woman of a sorrowful spirit: I have drunk neither wine nor strong drink, but have poured out my soul before the Lord. Count not thine handmaid for a daughter of Belial: for out of the abundance of my complaint and grief have I spoken hitherto.

Then Eli answered and said, go in peace: and the God of Israel grant thee thy petition that thou hast asked of Him. And she said, let thine handmaid find grace in thy sight. So the woman went her way, and did eat, and her countenance was no more sad. And they rose up in the morning early, and worshipped before the Lord, and returned, and came to their house to Ramah: and Elkanah knew Hannah his wife; and the Lord remembered her. Wherefore it came to pass, when the time was come about after Hannah had conceived, that she bare a son, and called his name Samuel, saying, because I have asked him of the Lord."

Hannah's prayer clearly came to pass. God revealed a few things to me during my study time of these scriptures. First, Hannah was upset with God. The scripture says she had bitterness in her soul when she went before God, but she still prayed and wept (supplicated) unto the Lord. God knew her heart and spoke to her through Eli, the prophet, telling her that God heard her cry and would answer her prayer. And God did. Samuel was born!

This was ordained in her life, and Hannah believed by faith when praying. After she prayed, she waited until it came to pass. We need to learn to do the same. If you are reading and feel you are at this place as well, wait patiently upon the Lord. What you believe shall come to pass in due season, according to His will.

These examples of answered prayers show that effective praying does result in answered prayers. Moses, Elias, and Hannah all prayed with a sincere heart, had a connection with God, a genuine, intimate relationship with God, and *selfless* hearts.

Moses' relationship with God was so close that God repented (changed His mind) when he approached Him. If we can get a revelation of the degree and level of this relationship with God, we also could have the privilege of God repenting and changing His mind about the outcome of a situation that concerns us if it aligns with His Word and His will. God's Word says that He is not respecter of persons, and if we have a genuine close relationship with Him also, based on the situation, what He did for Moses, He will do for us.

Think, pray, and meditate about what you have read. Seek God's face for the answers. Stay in the covenant of God and follow all His commandments. This, along with focusing on God and pleasing Him, is part of effective praying and answered prayers. I recommend that you read all of James 5 for further understanding.

I pray that the Holy Spirit reveals key factors about answered prayers that will enhance your prayer life and help it become more effective.

Chapter Sixteen: The Effects of Praying at an Appointed Time

On the days that I do not take time to honor God first and pray, my day starts off with many challenges. I fail to correctly react to the problems, so I don't respond with wisdom, peace, strength, revelation, and joy. When we take the time to start our day with prayer, we have the privilege and honor of being filled with wisdom, peace, strength, revelation, joy, and fellowship with our Heavenly Father, which is essential in our daily walk with God.

I have learned that it is worth losing sleep, slowing down, and honoring God rather than going through trials, tribulation, or misfortune without God's wisdom, peace, strength, revelation, joy, and fellowship. Do not get me wrong, I still experience the same challenges, but my response involves peace, strength, and joy, which makes a different regarding my outcome.

My heart's desire is that each of you experience and grab hold of what God has for you. Once again, you can discover this by developing a relationship with God and spending time with Him in prayer, reading, and meditation on His Word.

I also believe that to know God is to explore His being, which also happens by reading His Word. As we read His Word, we will become accustomed to pray without ceasing (communicating with God always), which allows us to become aware of our purpose and stay focused on righteousness. Let's not allow prayer time to pass us by. Let us be in constant prayer, believing that whatever comes against us, God has already directed or orchestrated the outcome, and we can stay in our place of peace and joy! Remember, we have the victory.

Let's not allow the opportunity to pray for others when prompted to pass us by either. The very moment that the person or persons come to mind, you should stop and pray on their behalf, praying a hedge of protection over the person or persons. Most importantly, pray whatever the Holy Spirit places on your heart for them.

As I have put God first in my life no matter what comes up, I have experienced fewer disappointments. If you are not putting God first; or if you are struggling to put Him first, just try it for a few days. I assure you, you will not be disappointed. Hopefully, you will be able to add more days so that it eventually becomes part of your daily routine. For He knows all things, and when we go before Him, seeking His face first daily, He reveals Himself in our walk in ways that will cause us to be in awe of Him.

Chapter Seventeen: Spiritual Warfare: Prayer and Intercession

The Bible says that we "wrestle not against flesh and blood, but against principalities against powers, against rulers of the darkness of this world and against spiritual wickedness in high places" (Ephesians 6:12).

Warring is a form of prayer. Dictionary.com defines war as conflict, which is a struggle, battle, or a state of opposition.[1] The words that stand out to me the most in this definition are a struggle or clash between opposing forces. This definitely lines up with the previous scripture, which addresses a fight against opposing forces. If we are righteous, the opposing force is evil. The scripture does not say that we *pray* against principalities, against powers, so forth and so on, but that we *fight* against them. There is a difference. How do we accomplish this? God's Word can be used to fight off opposing forces that daily come against us. As previously mentioned, "the Word of God is quick, powerful and sharper than a two edged sword" (Hebrews 4:12). The definition of quicken in this scripture means to give or restore or stir up. [2]

I had to learn that the person before me causing so much chaos, challenging me, and sometimes even succeeding in pulling me from my connection with God was not the actual person in the flesh but forces of darkness using that person. You see, we must know who the true enemy is when we are on the battlefield. We must learn to identify the enemy in order to be successful and effective in interceding and winning the war. Matthew 18:18 says, "Whatsoever ye shall bind on earth shall be bound in heaven: and whatsoever ye shall loose on earth shall be loosed in heaven." According to Wikipedia, bind and loose in the Bible simply means to forbid by an indisputable authority and to permit by an indisputable authority.[3] I have learned that most situations are battles between darkness (evil) and light (good). I bind up the darkness of evil running rampant, and loosen the righteousness of God over the situation.

The origin of the word war in Hebrew comes from the word *tsaba* which, according to the Strong's Concordance means army, war, or warfare.[4] The definition of warfare is armed conflict between two massed enemies or armies.[5] This definition is to the point. Of course, the enemy is Satan. So it is evident that we are dealing with forces of good and forces of evil on a day-to-day basis. We must fight, war, and press into victory!

If we understand this, we need to consistently position ourselves for warfare daily. Ephesians 6:10–18 instructs us, "Be strong in the Lord, and in the power of His might. Put on the whole armour of God that ye may be able to stand against the wiles of the devil.

For we wrestle not against flesh and blood, but against

principalities, against powers, against the rulers of the darkness of this world, against spiritual wickedness in high places. Wherefore take unto you the whole armour of God that ye may be able to withstand in the evil day, and having done all, to stand. Stand therefore, having your loins girt about with *truth*, and having on the breastplate of *righteousness*; and your feet shod with the preparation of the gospel of *peace*; above all, taking the shield of *faith*, wherewith ye shall be able to quench all the fiery darts of the wicked. And take the helmet of *salvation*, and the sword of the *Spirit*, which is *the Word of God*: *Praying always* with all prayer and supplication in the spirit, and watching thereunto with all perseverance and supplication for all saints" (emphasis added).

These passages bring awareness that we are dressing ourselves for protection against the darkness of the world we face each day. We go before the Lord, receiving His *power* and *might* as we dress ourselves to war against the forces of darkness, prepare to pray, and spend time in God's presence to start off our day. We invite the Holy Spirit, the revelator, to help us in prayer. We pray God's truth, position ourselves to enter into His righteousness, and set ourselves in a place of peace.

We pray God's Word for the solution of our circumstances, believing by faith that God will hear and answer according to His will, knowing we have His salvation. He will save us from the enemy and plant our feet on solid ground, sustaining us and walking us into victory of the concerns on our hearts as we pray in Jesus's name!

Putting on the *armor of God* daily has changed my life and the outcome of my circumstances. This has helped me to understand that everything in the Bible is for my use, keeping me focused on being in the world but not of the world.

Ephesians 6 states that we must deal with fiery darts of wickedness in high places. We must be on guard and prepared to press through whatever forces come against us including the cares of the world. Often, we must war against conflicts. We all need to understand warfare, its importance during prayer, and how to overcome in this season.

We need more believers who have a genuine, intimate relationship with God standing in the gap, on the wall, travailing, praying, and warring so that we can witness the manifestation of 2 Chronicles 7:14 in the earth and see it come to pass. "If my people, which are called by my name, shall *humble* themselves, and *pray*, and *seek my face*, and *turn from their wicked ways*; then will I hear from heaven, and will forgive their sin, and will heal their land" (emphasis added).

Are you willing to be the one (a righteous one) to go before God, stand in the gap, intercede, war if you must, and claim victory over this land to follow our Lord of Lords and walk in righteousness?

I go before God daily when I awake and seek Him. I make sure to stay in His covenant and in His perfect will. I decree and declare His covenant and promises in my life. When I do these things daily, I have a better outlook on life and can put the cares of the world into a Godly perspective.

This is not to say that I do not face snares and traps. I still do, but my approach is different. I pull down the strongholds through prayer, otherwise known as warring, I make it a point to always connect to God, our "I AM."

We must be able to determine the situation, which the Holy Spirit reveals to us when we are connected with God. Some circumstances are just life situations. But no matter the situation, God's written Word has the answer. We should all learn to always use God's Word to get us through each day. Prayer can take a situation and turn it around by the mercy and grace of God.

We give Him thanks. We decree and declare His goodness and mercy for the victory. Decree means to command or ordain. When you are praying in the spirit and praying with the Holy Spirit, you are connected with God. Then when you speak words of your known tongue in prayer, you can feel confident to decree because you have tapped into the supernatural. The Holy Spirit is praying through you and guiding you while your provisions are being transitioned into the natural realm.

According to dictionary.com, the definition of decree is one of the eternal purposes of God, by which events are foreordained, a formal and authoritative order.[6] In the dictionary, declare means to make known or state clearly.[7] The meaning of affirm is to confirm or maintain as true what you have prayed and the scriptures you have read that led to the resolution spoken over the situation.[8] You declare by the power within you when you received the Holy Spirit by God's mercy, and it shall come to pass.

Let us understand that we can only decree and declare by the power of the Holy Ghost (Holy Spirit) within us. "Ye shall receive power, after that the Holy Ghost comes upon you . . ." (Acts 1:8a)

Job 22:28 states, "Thou shalt also *decree* a thing, and it shall be established *unto thee*: and the light shall shine upon thy ways" (emphasis added). Job's stance with God permitted him the power to declare this decree.

The scripture says that it shall be established unto thee, referring to Job, and the light shall shine upon Job's ways.

The word established means to bring about permanently.[9] Do you feel you are at a place with God to declare and decree and establish like Job did?

The Holy Spirit comes with power, which gives us authority to position ourselves by faith to *decree* and *declare* things to materialize in our lives in due season that we are expecting from God if we have a genuine relationship with Him and in aligned with His will.

The person making the decree must be in a position of power and authority to do so. Once I understood this scripture, I had to believe by faith that I had the power and authority to make a decree and by faith, expect that it would be carried out, according to God's purpose and plan. In other words, I decreed and declared by faith that it shall come to pass in the natural realm. When praying, you have the right to decree and declare. For those who have received the activation of the Holy Spirit abiding in you, you have the power within you—Holy Ghost power!

Also when you decree and declare, believe it will be established. Again, established means to bring about what has been spoken.

Always remember, we *must put on our armor of God daily* in order to always be prepared to stand against the wiles (deception) of the enemy in our lives daily.

---

1. "Warring," dictionary.com, accessed September 7, 2018, https://www.dictionary.com/browse/warring?s=t.
2. "Quicken," dicitionary.com, accessed September 7, 2018, https://www.dictionary.com/browse/quicken?s=t.
3. "Binding and Loosing," wikipedia.com, accessed September 7, 2018, https://en.wikipedia.org/wiki/Binding_and_loosing.
4. "Tsaba," biblestudytools.com, accessed September 7, 2018, https://www.biblestudytools.com/lexicons/hebrew/kjv/tsaba-2.html.

5. "Warfare," dictionary.com, accessed September 7, 2018, https://www.dictionary.com/browse/warfare?s=t.

6. "Decree," dictionary.com, accessed September 7, 2018, https://www.dictionary.com/browse/decree?s=t.

7. "Declare," dictionary.com, accessed September 7, 2018, https://www.dictionary.com/browse/declare?s=t.

8. "Affirm," dictionary.com, accessed September 7, 2018, https://www.dictionary.com/browse/affirm?s=t.

9. "Establish," dictionary.com, accessed September 7, 2018, https://www.dictionary.com/browse/establish?s=t.

Chapter Eighteen: A Review of the Characteristics of an Intercessor

Now that you are almost finished reading this book, have you stopped yet to ask yourself if you are called as an intercessor or prayer warrior? Or have you heard a still, soft voice saying, "I have called you to be an intercessor or a prayer warrior?"

I hope that by now, you have realized how important it is to establish a deep relationship with God so that you can succeed in your calling as an intercessor.

This book is entitled *A Call to Intercession*, which gives you an idea of my calling as an intercessor. One of my greatest discoveries was realizing that there is more to prayer than what meets the eye. After experiencing and receiving this revelation, I felt led to write this book and share my experiences, beliefs about prayer, and my revelation with others. I have received these insights about prayer from the Holy Spirit while being developed as an intercessor.

I realized that fulfilling my calling as an intercessor is

more than picking out scriptures, reading, and praying them on Sunday morning. It is instead a duty and a calling of importance that can even be a matter of life or death in some cases—the difference between someone's soul being lost or saved. It can be a matter of whether the church congregation encounters God's manifested presence during a gathering and even experiencing God's manifested presence at levels of expectancy and witnessing His glory. I do not want to belittle anyone who prays in any way or any setting, but intercessors are also known to set the tone and atmosphere for God's manifested presence. God has given intercessors the responsibility for other people in many ways you might not be aware of, and you want to always make sure you are hearing from God. Allow Him to use you and submit to the Holy Spirit. Sanction the Holy Spirit to pray with and through you to always accomplish God's will, not yours, when praying for others.

As mentioned earlier, any person can pray, but please understand that not everyone who prays is an intercessor. The key is the life and heart of the person when praying. An intercessor always stands in the gap for others, going before God, seeking mercy for those they are praying for as opposed to judgment. They are willing to take a risk and sacrifice in order to obtain mercy. They are not told to pray for someone; it is an automatic response. Their heart's desire is to pray for those in need, seldom praying for their own needs. A true intercessor hears and sees through the eyes of God. Prayer and kind deeds go hand and hand for intercessors.

Intercessors are broken men and women of God. "He who comes before the Lord must have a broken spirit and a heart" (Psalm 51:17).

Intercessors do not always operate in open view, but they most often work in the background or behind closed doors. They allow God to use them to intercede and pray on behalf of His people. They are *called* and *chosen* by God and focused on living a righteous and holy life.

They are great givers of their money and time. And believe it or not, intercessors can change the mind of God as referenced earlier.

Intercessors are called by God to intercede for God's people. Are you being called? Have you been called and ignored the call? Or you have been called but failed to fulfill the call because of the required sacrifice?

THE TIME IS NOW!

Chapter Nineteen: Intercessor Self-Test

Are you Person A or Person B?

Persons A does what is right because they know God and have a genuine relationship with Him. The persons know God truly loves and cares for them and is merciful in spite of any failures in life. Therefore, the persons want to do what is right, because the persons have been conformed to the image and likeness of Christ. The persons hate the things God hates and loves the things God loves.

Persons B believe that they are the only ones whose life and heart has been transformed by the love and power of Christ. Persons B believe Persons A has not been transformed on the inside of the heart. If fear and brownie points are taken away it is hard to tell where their heart would be or if it would be Christ like.

I believe that God wants to take us to a special place in Him, and while on the journey, we will have a desire to want to do what is right. This desire can only come from a genuine relationship with Him! We should intimately *know* His goodness (not just read about it), so we can truly repent of our failures wholeheartedly. God's Word tells us that it is His goodness that leads a person to true repentance.

God searches the heart of man, and in order to enter God's presence during prayer, we must enter in *spirit and truth*. We must have holy hands and a pure heart, which we receive through repentance and being forgiven of sin. For a better understanding and revelation of repentance, I highly recommend reading all of Romans 2 and asking the Holy Spirit for insight. I believe you will be enlightened.

Summary of the Self-Test

An intercessor has matured to a place of seeing and hearing through the eyes of our God. They view the world from God's perspective and will have a burning desire with the burden of becoming an intercessor. Read Nehemiah 1:1–5 for more information.

- Do you allow God to use you for His own benefit when praying? If your answer is yes, how often do you pray to God on behalf of others versus praying about your needs and; or your immediate family concerns?
- Do you see situations or people in predicaments that break your heart, and you began to tear up or cry? What breaks God's heart should break an intercessor's heart, and this is the place where true intercession begins.
- Ezekiel 9:4–5 indicates that intercessors are

marked by God. Has anyone ever prophesied and told you that God has called you to become an intercessor? Have they indicated that you have a prayer mantle? Do they see you always praying for others, forsaking your own needs?

- Are you at a point in your life where all you want to do is please God and lead a disciplined and holy life?

I believe, as intercessors, God will not hear our prayer (communication) if we are living in or hiding unconfessed sins in our lives.

As previously stated, intercessors are not normally instruments of prayer operating in open view. They work best in the background or behind closed doors. I am not saying that intercessors do not pray openly because we do. But I personally, prefer praying in secret. When I asked God why I felt this way, He led me to scriptures and research to explain this. I found a questionnaire online that answered my questions so that I finally understood my prayer life much better.

I hope this book does the same for you: helps you understand your role and position as a called intercessor in this season so that you have insight into others that might also be called as *intercessors*. You can intercede and pray for them.

Conclusion

The Hebrew word for abundance is *shefa*. In contrast, the opposite of this is lack. God intends for each of us to have fullness in life and abundance as stated in John 10:10b. In order to live a life of abundance, we have a roadmap to follow that includes the laws and commands of God in His written Word.

According to the Hebrew definition, joy is related to abundance. God's Word says, "The joy of the Lord is our strength" (Nehemiah 8:10b). This is part of the roadmap I mentioned above that must be followed to obtain abundance. How do we receive joy and strength? Being in God's presence brings joy, and we will receive strength to endure life on this earth and become steadfast, walking into a life of abundance. You might wonder about this. Nehemiah 8:10 referenced above further explains this. "He said unto them, Go your way, eat the fat, and drink the sweet, and send portions unto them for whom nothing is prepared: for this day is holy unto our Lord: neither be ye sorry; for the joy of the Lord is your strength."

Therefore, instructions regarding intercession and intercessors are specified in God's Word. Since we are talking about prayer and intercession, the verse, "pray without ceasing" comes to mind (1 Thessalonians 5:17). Many Christians and believers take this tiny verse lightly. At one point in my Christian walk, I did as well. But we need to take it seriously. As I have repeated throughout this book, prayer (praying) is communication with God. "Praying without ceasing" means to always communicate with God. The definition of without means with the absence, lacking.[1] Prayer should be present during our daily activities. To cease means to bring or come to an end. Never stop communicating with God.

As individual believers and Christians, we should always be in a position to communicate with God. In the beginning, after the heavens and earth were created, God created Adam and then Eve and placed them in the Garden of Eden so that He could communicate with them daily. He is the same yesterday, today, and forevermore. He wants to have this same intimate communion with Christians and believers today: daily communication. As I write the conclusion of this book, I see a vision of a man and woman sitting and waiting on God to make His appearance in the Garden so that they can spend time together and communicate with Him. This pertains to each of us!

We should seek a divine relationship with our Heavenly Father and His son as we are transformed into righteous people. This will lead us into the gateway of the wealthy place. Daily we will be entering God's presence in the secret place, the dwelling place, past the outer courts, into the inner courts, and going behind the veil.

As for the church, let us understand that spiritual travailing in prayer is vital to birth spiritual people in the Body of Christ. Galatians 4:19 tells us, "God's little children, of whom He travail in birth again until Christ be formed in them."

Travail means to labor with pain.[2] Most women probably associate the term "labor with pain when giving natural birth to a child or children, but this also means to labor daily in our Christian walk into righteousness.

At times, I must press in to maintain righteousness daily, and most often, it is intense labor and quite painful, to be honest. I call it being afflicted, which is *anah* in Hebrew.[3] The meaning of afflicted in Hebrew is to abase self or defile.

As a mom who naturally birthed two children through labor, suffering and hardship exists both naturally and spiritually. We can easily give into the cares of the world. We are not born-again creations made to run from righteousness but to run toward righteousness. After we received Jesus Christ as our Savior, we were freed from a world of darkness and the related associations.

We are born again as new creations in Christ Jesus when we received salvation. In Him is victory. We are heirs, joint heirs, with Christ Jesus, sons and daughters of God. As a new creation, we have the same DNA as Jesus within us. The definition of DNA is the fundamental and distinctive characteristics or qualities of someone, especially when regarded as unchangeable.[4] In John 15:1–5, Jesus says, "I am the true vine, and my Father is the husbandman. Every branch in me that beareth not fruit he taketh away: and every branch that beareth fruit, He purgeth it, that it may bring forth more fruit. Now ye are clean through the Word which I have spoken unto you. Abide in Me, and I in you. As the branch cannot bear fruit of itself, except it abide in the vine; no more can ye, except ye abide in me. I am the vine, ye are the branches: He that abideth in me, and I in Him, the same bringeth forth much fruit: for without me ye can do nothing."

We must understand that we are part of the Body of Christ. We are contributors and have a responsibility to the Body of Christ to join forces with others regardless of their denomination as long their teaching lines up with the Word of the True Living God; being of one mind, one body, and one accord to experience the fullness of God's glory on this earth. We are to go out into the world and tell others about the glory of the True Living God, His goodness, and His mercy. This is what it means to preach the gospel.

The process begins through intercession (prayer) and believing that it will come to pass. We all have an obligation to God as believers to strive to be in His perfect will, to stand and walk in righteousness! We cannot compromise or straddle the fence. It is necessary that we choose to become committed to the purpose and plan of God for our lives—not our will, but His *will*.

Once God commands something or someone to be part of our life, no one can change or stop it. When we pray and when God has commanded it, it cannot be undone. But when we say we are led, we need to make sure we are led by the Holy Spirit.

Personally, I don't want to continue to mess up, so I have been asking God to make His ways evident to me so that I will not trip up. I want His will to be evident in my life. I ask that it be so illogical that I will definitely know it is

Him, because He is *not* logical at all. This assures me there will be no way possible that it is man's doing because of how it unfolds in the natural realm. This is to make sure God and only God receives the glory.

We must grab ahold of the revelation of the importance of prayer and intercession and allow the Holy Spirit to develop our technique of praying. We must pay it forward, pass along the revelation, and teach and develop others how to become effective intercessors and prayer warriors to pursue God's plan. Our goal should be to save the lost and lead them into the revelation of truth. Praying for the lost emphasizes the importance of prayer and intercession. We understand how prayer can and should be used in our daily walk as a new creation in Christ Jesus to become victorious. Awareness of prayer keeps us in relation with God while on earth once we accept Jesus Christ as Lord and Savior and are filled with the Holy Spirit. Thank you, Jesus, for this revelation!

Lord, let your light shine, revealing unto all the following people—the lost, the backslider and the compromiser—that there is an answer, and His name is *Jesus*.

I Pray Blessings Upon You All!

1. "Without," dictionary.com, accessed September 7, 2018, https://www.dictionary.com/browse/without?s=t.
2. "Travail," dictionary.com, accessed September 7, 2018, https://www.dictionary.com/browse/travail?s=t.
3. "anah," biblehub.com, accessed September 7, 2018, https://biblehub.com/hebrew/anah.htm#.
4. "DNA," oxforddictionaries.com, accessed September 7, 2018, https://en.oxforddictionaries.com/definition/dna.

Dear Reader:

After reading the book, if your goal and desire is to establish an intimate relationship with God or elevate your intimate relationship, become an intercessor, participate in intercession, pray, and receive answered prayers, I would like to share this advice that I believe will be helpful in reaching your goal:

- Pursue entering into God's presence by seeking His kingdom and His righteousness first every day. (Matthew 6:33) This initiates awareness of our Heavenly Father, Jesus, and the Holy Spirit.
- Dress in the "Armour of God" in order to be protected from the attacks of the enemy. (Ephesians 6:11-18) This also affords you with the ability to stay in alignment with the Trinity: God, the Father, Jesus, the Son, and the Holy Spirit throughout the day.
- Acknowledge who you are in Christ Jesus and be led by the Holy Spirit daily. (Romans 8:1-16)
- Receive your spiritual nourishment (your daily bread) (Matthew 6:11). Allow yourself to learn who God is to you by reading His Word. If you are not accustomed to reading the Bible daily or regularly, start by reading a scripture a day. Eventually, you will read more as time evolves.
- Always humble yourself, pray, seek God's face, and repent of sin, iniquity, and transgression. This pleases God.

I trust as you continue this course, you will hunger, thirst and yearn to become closer to God and it will elevate your prayer life and your relationship with Him, Jesus, and the Holy Spirit.

Prayer For Believers

Father, I come before you with a humble heart. I submit myself unto your authority, and I ask that you bend your ear and hear my prayer on behalf of my sisters and brothers in Christ. I pray that we all will continue to develop a genuine, intimate relationship with you. I pray that we stay connected to you so that you can lead us into your perfect will through the Holy Spirit, who teaches and guides us when we submit ourselves unto you.

In our time of worship, in your presence, reveal to us the things to come, your purpose and plan for our lives. Let us not turn away and fight against your will, but submit our will to your will in Jesus's name. Help us understand who you are to us so that we may be true witnesses to the lost, allowing them to see your glory upon us while drawing the lost to us as we draw near to you.

We need your power and strength, your grace and mercy, to be released within us to do your perfect will. Through prayer, we will seek your face, honor your direction and carry it out as you have purposed in this season In Jesus's name.

We decree and declare this prayer, believing it is done. We thank

You, Lord, for hearing our prayer and answering in Jesus's mighty name. We decree and declare your Word in John 15:7. "If we abide in you, and your word abide in us, we shall ask what we will, and it shall be done unto us," knowing Your Word shall not return void In Jesus's name, Amen. Selah!

If you become weak in your faith and you are pulled into a slump, and doubt arises; if you have prayed prayers and they have not been answered yet, remember God answered your prayer for salvation. He really does answer prayers, according to His will, His purpose, and plan for our lives!

If you are not sure of your salvation, please pray this prayer along with me.

PRAYER OF SALVATION

Dear Lord, I am a sinner, and I ask for your forgiveness. I believe Jesus died for my sins and rose from the dead. As of this day, I will trust and follow you as my Lord and Savior Jesus. Fill me with the Holy Spirit and I pray you will allow the Holy Spirit to guide my life and help me to do your will.

Lord, I acknowledge you as the Trinity: God, the Father; the Son; and the Holy Spirit. It is written in First John 5:7, "there are three that bear record in heaven, the Father, the Word in the Flesh [Jesus Christ] and the Holy Ghost; and these three are one."

God, your written Word says in John 3:16 that "You so loved the world that you gave your only begotten Son, [Jesus Christ] that whoever believeth in Him should not perish, but have everlasting [eternal] life." We all have done, thought, or said bad things, which the Bible calls sin. The written Word says, "All have sinned and come short of the glory of God" (Romans 3:23). "But, Jesus died and we have been bought with a price so that we could have a relationship with You, God and be with you forever."

I know I cannot earn salvation, but I am saved by your grace, if I have faith in Your Son, Jesus Christ. In Jesus's Name. Amen.

About the Author

God ignited a passion for intercession within Arnester when she was awakened one night in 2006, and He spoke to her about this calling. In 2010, God moved her to a new church to develop and mature in her gift. She then began teaching a class on prayer and intercession. She later received a prophecy about the growth of her ministry through her involvement with the intercessory prayer team.

She believes that people should be known by their service and love toward others, and not by their titles. She has developed a ministry which includes prayer workshops, saving the lost, feeding the hungry, serving the poor, widows, and children and much more.

When she is not consulting or involved in ministry, Arnester enjoys spending her free time with her family. She also enjoys reading, playing the keyboards, writing worship songs, and, of course, praying.

If you feel called to be an intercessor after reading this book, or in need of prayer, please feel free to visit heartmattersministry.org and leave your contact information and someone will contact you.

Part of the proceeds from book sale will be donated to Safe house, 89 Ellis St.NE, Atlanta, Ga 30303. Phone: 404-835-8891, www.safehouseoutreach.org. A non-profit organization responsible for all programs and service actions for those experiencing *"homelessness"* and Sword of the Lord Churches, Int'l, *"a place of worship"*, 2810 Church Street, East Point, GA 30344. Phone: 404-625-9116.

Arnester will be releasing her next book *"21 Day Financial Fast"* in 2020. For a launch date feel free to visit the link below:

heartmattersministry.org

Printed in Great Britain
by Amazon

49683000R00087